BENNY'S BOYS

THE STABLE OF BENNY JACOBS

WYNFORD JONES

BENNY'S BOYS
THE STABLE OF BENNY JACOBS

First published in Great Britain in 2007 by
Wynford Jones
3 Sycamore Close,
Aberdare

Printed and bound by
Colourplan Design & Print
St. Helens
Merseyside

A catalogue record for this book
is available from the British Library.

ISBN 978-0-9551082-1-1

Contents

Acknowledgements

I am grateful to Harry Carroll and Lennie Williams for their patience in answering my questions relating to their time as members of Benny`s stable and I would also like to thank Dai Corp, Don James and Johnny Lewis for all their help.

Most of Benny`s boxers had their photographs taken at Craely Studios and I have used many of these excellent pictures but I must also thank Gordon Blakey, (especially for the photo which forms the basis of the cover design), David Hughes, Brian Renney, Bill Holder, Dave Furnish and the "Royal Oak" for lending me their photographs. Thanks are also due to Mark Warner for the loan of programmes.

I am also grateful to the Western Mail and South Wales Echo for the use of photographs and I would like to thank Saffron Herbert and Tina Auckbarally of the Photosales Department for their help while all quotations from those newspapers have been duly acknowledged.

Thanks are also due to the staff of the Local Studies Department of Cardiff Central Library who were extremely helpful with my queries.

I would particularly like to thank Gareth and his staff at Victoria Studios, Aberdare for all their help with photographic material and while every effort has been made to acknowledge copyright I can only apologise in cases where it has not been possible to establish the copyright holder.

Thanks go to Claude Abrams, the editor of Boxing News for permission to quote from past editions and whose record books and annuals proved to be invaluable in compiling the career records of all the boxers featured in the book.

Finally, I would like to thank the staff at Colourplan, and Brian Meadows for all his help in ensuring that yet another of my projects becomes a reality.

Introduction

Following the successful launch of my first book "Class of the 60s", the stable of Eddie Thomas, I was invited to the London Ex-Boxers` Association annual awards lunch in February, 2006 and as I entered the hall, LEBA member Chas Taylor shouted across to me that he had the title for my next book. When I asked Chas what he had in mind, he replied: "Benny`s Boys".

At the time I was more concerned with enjoying my day in London, but over the following days and weeks I began to think more and more about the suggestion. Having grown up in Merthyr Tydfil I had spent a great deal of time in the company of boxers from Eddie`s stable, but even then I was aware of the rivalry with Benny Jacobs, Mac Williams and the Cardiff boys and there was clearly a story to tell.

Benny was always in the news and so were his boxers. He must have spent hours on the telephone to local and national journalists thereby ensuring that his ever-growing stable of fighters got acres of newspaper coverage. Significantly, this guaranteed them work and as Benny`s negotiating skills developed, each of his boxers earned well.

I look on boxing as an ongoing tapestry, but the quality of the tapestry is coloured by the characters and fighters which make up this great sport. There is no question that Benny was one of boxing`s great characters and he built up a fine stable of fighters. Surprisingly, Joe Erskine was his only champion, but his stable included several fighters of championship class and these, along with the ones who slipped into the role of "journeymen fighter", without whom the sport could not exist, have all contributed to a remarkable period when boxing was rarely out of the news.

"Benny`s Boys" is their story. I have taken the boxers I regard as the core of the stable and each has a chapter, together with photographs and complete record, while the final section of the book includes selected records of fighters looked after by Benny over the years.

Chapter 1

Benny Jacobs was born in Bute Street, Cardiff on June 13th, 1912. Growing up in the dock area of the city he attended Howardian High School, where he was taught by Rhys Gabe, the Welsh international rugby centre. He came from a sporting family with his brother Nat becoming a swimmer of Olympic standard. Benny himself loved rugby and would eventually travel to Paris and Dublin regularly for international matches.

As a young man he worked in a solicitor`s office for a time before deciding that the law was not for him and even worked for a time as a lather-boy. He always lived in the city before eventually settling in Penarth with his wife, Rose who maintained that being married to Benny was great fun and that there was never a dull moment!

He developed a passion for greyhound racing and he was frequently to be seen at the Arms Park dog track and at many other South Wales venues. He was also a bookmaker and he had been involved in boxing for over thirty years when he died, at the age of 69, on October 30th, 1981.

The headquarters of Benny`s operation was his gym in Custom House Street. Known as "England`s", taking the name of the fruit and vegetable merchant occupying the ground floor, his betting shop was located on the second floor, and since these were frowned upon by the law, the venture was manned by one of his business associates. The gym itself was located on the third floor, and this was where Benny held court.

During his time in boxing he managed many of Wales` finest fighters and was rarely out of the news. For many years he commissioned personalised cartoon - like Christmas cards featuring members of his stable and listing each of his fighters at that point in time, and he once said, "If my boys get the publicity and the fights why should I worry what my enemies call me?"

At the beginning of his managerial career he was looking after the likes of David "Darkie" Hughes, Phil Edwards, Teddy Best and Joe Erskine. Joe became British and Empire Heavyweight Champion while "Darkie" and Phil challenged Dave Charnley and Terry Downes respectively for their titles. Later, he would go on to steer Harry Carroll and Lennie "The Lion" Williams into British title challenges while towards the end of his life he managed flyweight Kelvin Smart and heavyweight Rudi Pika before handing them over to Mickey Duff when his health began to fail, thus ensuring that his boys would have the best of opportunities with Mickey, who, at the time was arguably the most influential person on the fight scene in Britain.

Sadly, Benny did not live to see Kelvin Smart become British Flyweight Champion while the life of Rudi Pika ended in tragic circumstances.

Benny was undoubtedly a Runyonesque character and from my first meeting with him at a promotion at the Miners` Hall in Merthyr in 1961, the one thing that stands out in my mind was his sense of humour. He enjoyed being the centre of attention and was obviously great fun to be with.

For many years he was one of the main men in Welsh boxing. He served on the Welsh Area Council of the British Boxing Board of Control as a managers` representative and later held the position of Chairman. Stories abound in relation to his friendships and feuding with managerial rivals Mac Williams and Eddie Thomas but he brought humour and colour to the position of chairman and there are numerous tales of things getting out of hand and virtually coming to blows at times, though there is no doubt that boxing was thriving in Wales at the time.

He never really gave up his involvement in the sport and even on the night before he died Benny had been present at a Welsh Area Council meeting at the Royal Hotel in Cardiff to support an application for a manager`s licence from Teddy Best, one of his protégés.

Though confined to a wheelchair in his later years, Benny frequently appeared at ringside, usually brought along by Joe Erskine, and my final memory of Benny is of seeing him with Joe at the Ebbw Bridge Social Club in Newport when I refereed there in June, 1981, with Benny enjoying a "rum and black" before the boxing began.

Following his death there were countless tributes and Ray Parker, in the South Wales Echo wrote: "British Boxing – and Wales in particular – has lost one of its greatest characters with the death of Benny Jacobs".

Karl Woodward, writing in the Western Mail ran with the headline, "Benny`s boys pay tribute to a real character." He went on to refer to Benny`s service with the RAF in Eritrea, North Africa where he developed a reputation as the Squadron "scrounger" and some of his friends remain convinced that the character of Sergeant Bilko was based on him!

The tributes to Benny are quite revealing in seeking out the real person. Mr D.S.Davies, a former referee and Chairman of the Welsh Area Council said: "He was always a good man to his boxers and had some of Wales` greatest under his management".

Dave Phillips, Secretary of the Welsh Area Council and a former Echo boxing correspondent who knew Benny extremely well described him as "the number one character in British boxing." He went on: "He was a great ad-libber and I`m sure there have been more stories relating to Benny than anyone else in the sport."

One such story concerns the complaint of a pressman that one of his boxers had been difficult to understand during an interview. Benny replied, "That's because I told him to keep his gumshield in.!"

In looking at what some of his former boxers said of him, David "Darkie" Hughes paid the following tribute: "Benny was the greatest. No matter what people say about him, you couldn`t fault him as far as his interest in his boxers was concerned.

The only people who put him down were those jealous of his success. He looked after his boxers and wouldn't take a penny from them until they were established.

He had the best stable in the country at his peak. He could turn nasty if you gave a bad performance but he really had a heart of gold. His death is the end of an era in Welsh boxing."

Former Welsh Lightweight Champion Teddy Best said: "Benny did his utmost for his boxers to get them good matches and obtain the best purses possible. He made an enormous contribution to the sport."

Mickey Duff paid tribute as follows: "Benny Jacobs was one of the wittiest men I ever met and in my opinion the best manager of boxers to come out of Wales in my time."

There are countless stories of Benny's generosity with both Harry Carroll and Lennie "The Lion" Williams giving examples of his care when they were injured and in need of prompt medical treatment, while Dennis Avoth, brother of former British and Empire Lightheavyweight Champion Eddie, provides another insight. He remembers travelling in to Cardiff on the bus as a young boy and meeting his father to go along to Benny's gym. Benny would always give him a half crown to buy chips on the way home, and later, as a young amateur boxer, Dennis tells of how well he was looked after by Benny when he would go along and take part in boxing exhibitions in local community halls and the Miners' Hospital.

He was a generous man and a great supporter of good causes. He was involved in staging an annual boxing tournament in aid of Jewish Youth Charities and Mr Emlyn Lewis, a plastic surgeon at the St. Lawrence Hospital, Chepstow frequently paid tribute to the way Benny would take his boxers along to their annual fund-raising fete and would work tirelessly on behalf of the cause.

Johnny Lewis, trainer of Dick Richardson, the former European Heavyweight Champion admired the fact that Benny would always be in the corner for his six-round fighters and would not farm this work out to others.

Ron Olver, long time contributor to Boxing News paid the following tribute to Benny as long ago as 1963, in his "Telefight News" column: "I rate Benny Jacobs as one of the shrewdest and most humane managers in the game today. He will not allow his boxers to take unnecessary punishment, and their welfare is always uppermost in his mind.

One of my most vivid memories of the Taylor/Williams bout is of Lennie struggling to beat the count, and Benny motioning to him as if to say "Stay down, son. You're too exhausted to get up. You'll live to fight another day."

Benny did cross swords with people, and one such person was former referee Joe Morgan. When I visited Joe in hospital following a hip-replacement operation he told of a meeting with Benny shortly before his death. Benny was seated in his wheelchair outside his home when along came Joe. They had not spoken for many years but as Joe approached, Benny was the first to speak. His words were: "Morgan, if you want to chat about old times, that's fine! But I don't want any of your bloody sympathy!"

Apart from being a shrewd businessman, Benny was also said to be proficient in several languages, including French, Italian, Arabic and Chinese. He was both a gourmet and an accomplished cook. When we couple this with his quick-wit and all the qualities which so many people have drawn attention to, it is clear that we have here a unique individual.

His funeral service was held at the Synagogue at Penylan in Cardiff and all his boxers turned out. This, in itself, was a remarkable tribute in a sport where falling out is a frequent occurrence. Not one of his boxers will have a bad word said about him, with each one of them emphasising how well they were treated. That, surely, is testimony that we are speaking of someone who was special to so many people.

JOE ERSKINE
British and Empire Heavy-weight Champion

Manager:
BENNY JACOBS

Trainer:
ARCHIE RULE

Benny Jacobs (left) with Joe Erskine & Archie Rule.
pic: the collection of David Furnish

Benny Jacobs (2nd left) with Joe Erskine (centre),
Gordon Blakey, Bernard Murphy & Phil Edwards.
pic: courtesy of Gordon Blakey

Christmas cards 'from Benny Jacobs & Stable'.
pics: from the collection of David Furnish

Kelvin Smart, the British Flyweight Champion, whose coronation Benny did not see.
pic: Wynford Jones

Chapter 2

Phil Edwards` first professional contest was against Fred Leek on October 28th, 1958 at the age of sixteen. The contest took place at Willenhall and Phil won on a knockout in the second round. His seventytwo fight career ended a decade later when he lost on points over ten rounds at Leicester to George Aldridge in an eliminator for the British Middleweight title.

During the intervening years Phil enjoyed remarkable success and most of his eight defeats came against boxers of championship class. After a successful start to his career, he notched up eighteen contests during 1953, losing just twice on points. Virtually every contest went the distance so he was gaining in experience all the time and a high level of fitness was guaranteed. Looking back over his workload, the words of Sugar Ray Robinson come to mind. He once said, "You never quit learning from the men you meet, whether you win, lose or draw." Journalist Tom Phillips of the Daily Herald and Cardiff matchmaker Harry Gorman were among those who were excited by Phil`s potential. He seemed to have everything. He was good looking, always appeared to be in peak physical condition and was always immaculately dressed, so much so that he was sometimes referred to as Beau Brummel. Harry Carroll and Lennie Williams both tell of how Benny`s Boys all went to one of Cardiff`s top tailors at the time, namely Goodfellow and French for their suits, but whereas most of them went along every six months, Phil would pick up new suits on a much more regular basis.

Trainer Archie Rule described Phil as a deliberate, "thinking" fighter but acknowledged he had genuine "box-office" appeal. Always concerned about his image he was almost obsessed with his hair looking perfect at all times.

He started his professional career with Eddie Dumazel but as with several of his stablemates soon moved to Benny`s gym. During the first two years of his career many of his contests took place at Willenhall Drill Hall and at Walsall Town Hall with a sprinkling of appearances in Cardiff. After beating Fred Balio on points in Cardiff on May 24th 1954 Phil was out of the ring for virtually two years in order to complete his National Service and he returned on April 17th, 1956 with a stoppage victory in the third round over Bob Jeacock at Birmingham. He went through the rest of the year unbeaten and in his first contest of 1957 he beat Noel Trigg on points over eight rounds in Cardiff. Contests followed in venues as far afield as Belle Vue, Manchester and Streatham Ice Rink and following his third round knockout of Paddy Delargy at

Abergavenny he was matched with Freddie Cross for the Welsh Middleweight Title. The contest was set for Pandy Park, Cross Keys on August 21st, 1957, and Phil took the title on points after twelve rounds.

The Edwards camp were confident and wanted a sidestake of £500. Freddie Cross weighed in at 11st. 3. 1/2lbs with Phil coming in about one pound heavier.

Up to the sixth round Cross was ahead on points though he was hard pressed to keep the younger man out. Cross slipped Phil's leads and had the experience to tie him up inside while Phil found Cross a difficult target.

The Abertillery man was floored in the eighth round and Phil forced the fight to the final bell making a huge effort to seal victory while Cross dodged and weaved out of trouble.

At the final bell referee Joe Morgan raised the arm of Phil Edwards as the winner after twelve torrid rounds, but ugly scenes followed as chairs were thrown. Swift action by the police prevented a full scale riot but referee Morgan had to be escorted from the ring while Benny Jacobs received a kick in the groin which had been aimed at the new champion by a disgruntled fan.

His next contest saw him matched with Dick Tiger at Sophia Gardens Pavilion on a Syd Wignall promotion on September 9th of the same year. Phil was beaten on points over ten rounds, but it was certainly no disgrace to lose to a man who had already beaten Terry Downes and who would go on to establish himself as one of boxing's all-time greats by winning the world middleweight title and the world lightheavyweight crown. Tiger's next two contests also took place in Cardiff and he did some of his training at Benny's gym. In October he beat Jean-Claude Poisson and in November he drew with Pat McAteer, both at Sophia Gardens and both contests were over ten rounds.

Dave Phillips covering the contest for the South Wales Echo attended the weigh-in at the Royal Hotel and described Phil as looking fit and confident as he scaled 11stone 6.1/2 pounds with Tiger holding a three pound weight advantage. His colourful account of the contest ran as follows: "That rugged wrecker of reputations, Dick Tiger, decisively outpointed Wales's pride and joy, twentyone year old middleweight champion Phil Edwards of Cardiff at Sophia Gardens Pavilion last night after ten of the roughest, toughest rounds seen locally since the days of the Rebecca Riots!

Make no mistake about it, referee Ike Powell's verdict at the end of this Man v Tiger jungle jamboree was the only possible one in the gory circumstances. Edwards tried to twist the tail of a man eater…… and got badly clawed for his pains.

Edwards, badly hampered by nose trouble which made breathing difficult in the later stages, never seemed to get going against the well muscled negro from Nigeria. Except for some spasmodic two-handed body punching he did little to halt the one way traffic of hooks and right crosses poured in by Tiger.

After a tentative start Tiger showed his claws in the second round when he brushed aside a left lead and connected with a crisp right to the jaw and followed it up with a left to the body.

Tiger took the third round with plenty to spare, landing repeatedly with jolting rights to head and body and outpunching the Cardiff man when they tangled inside.

As the fight progressed Tiger constantly demonstrated a liking for close work and mauled and slugged away sessions with devastating effect.

Edwards could never keep the fight at long distance where his superior left leading would have told.

Edwards improved in the fourth and caught Tiger with a left and right tattoo to the body and a left hook to the eye that brought a noticeable "mouse".

Edwards opened the sixth in heartening fashion. He gashed Tiger`s left eye after mid-ring brawling. Tiger tore in viciously in return and cut Edwards under the right eye. But the round was Edwards`s by a shade.

It was nip and tuck in the eighth with Edwards showing distress as he gulped air through his mouth and Tiger slammed in two-fisted.

The Cardiff fighter was hard-pressed, but never at any time in danger of being floored. He subdued Tiger with a smashing short right to the head that made him roll his eyes.

Edwards took the ninth with a surprising recovery. The last was a humdinger, with Edwards trying desperately to save the fight. He clipped Tiger with a short right to the chin and took a left hook to the body in return, but both men were obviously very tired.

Edwards was clearly outpointed, that is admitted, but it was not quite the one-sided thrashing some people would like to make it.

Tiger was the guv`nor inside and took advantage of some special knowledge of Edwards`s weaknesses from his one-time manager, Eddie Dumazel, who aided manager Tony Vairo in the corner, to make the Welsh champion look cumbersome and crude at times".

Dumazel was extremely bitter for many years regarding Phil`s departure for the Jacobs camp but some time before he died in April, 2003 there was an emotional re-union with Phil which was brought about by Dai Corp, a lifelong friend of Phil who had been managed by Eddie during his own professional career.

When he faced Tiger, Phil had clearly lacked snap and at times he was indeed, gasping for breath. After the contest, Benny insisted that he should go into hospital for an operation to clear his blocked nasal passages and after a holiday in New Zealand, he was ready for action once more.

Phil returned to winning ways stopping Lew Lazar in five rounds at Harringay Arena. Lazar, one of the famous family from Aldgate in London`s East End was an extremely experienced performer. In 1954 he boxed Wally Thom for the British and European Welterweight titles and in 1956 he boxed Pat McAteer for the middleweight title. Fight previews suggested that Lazar had recently abandoned his boxing skills in favour of a more physical approach, but Phil was more than able to cope with the Londoner`s tactics.

In February 1958, Phil travelled to Gothenburg with Joe Erskine who was facing Ingemar Johansson for the European Heavyweight Title. On the undercard, Phil was matched with Olle Bengtsson, a former opponent of Randolph Turpin who was beaten on points over ten rounds by the "Leamington Licker" in London. Phil beat Bengtsson on points and after returning home notched up another points victory over Jimmy Lynas at Birmingham.

On April 23rd, 1958 he beat Freddie Cross again on points over twelve rounds in a defence of his Welsh title but with the contest being recognised this time as an eliminator for the British Middleweight title.

The return took place at Sophia Gardens with Phil scaling 11st. 4.1/2 lbs and Freddie Cross coming in at 11st. 3lbs. This time, Phil was a convincing winner with Cross cut under the left eyebrow and boxing from memory in the last two rounds. He went on to stop Jean Barlet in London and on July 9th he beat Jean Ruellet on points at Coney Beach Arena, Porthcawl. This contest was on the undercard of a bill which saw Dick Richardson beat the American Bob Baker over ten rounds.

Phil`s big chance came on September 30th, 1958 when he was matched with Terry Downes, the British title having become vacant on the retirement of Pat McAteer. Downes had been hoping to meet McAteer for the title but following Pat`s retirement Promoter Jack Solomons stepped in with the Edwards match. The match was set for Harringay Arena which had special memories for Phil. He had boxed there as a schoolboy under the name of Phillip Celia, his father being Maltese. Lord Montgomery of Alamein was in attendance and was so impressed with Phil`s performance he took off his watch and presented it to him.

Top of the bill was Brian London against Willie Pastrano and Downes revelled in all the pre-fight hype. The boxers made their way to the ring to the sound of the familiar Solomons fanfare which was always far better than some of the more ridiculous ring-walks we have seen in recent years. Terry came to the ring believing that he could out-jab and out-punch Phil and that he could out-fight him if necessary but several journalists felt that Phil possessed the superior skills. On this occasion, Tom Phillips tipped against the talented Welshman on the basis that the Cardiff camp might adopt the wrong tactics against Downes, a colourful fighter who enjoyed a tear-up. Benny Jacobs and Phil doubted the ability of Downes, who had never gone beyond eight rounds, to last the fifteen round course and their plan was to let the Londoner use up all his energy and then take over in the later stages. Unfortunately, when it came time for Phil to go after his man in the seventh round he was unable to change gear, with Downes` attacks having taken so much out of him and Phil took a sustained beating until the contest was stopped by referee Bill Williams in the thirteenth round.

The newspapers were generous in their praise of Downes while the Daily Mail stated that Phil "had taken a hiding that had become almost too painful to watch".

Nat Fleischer, editor of the "Ring" magazine had been impressed by Phil Edwards and saw him as a future world title challenger but the defeats against Dick Tiger and Terry Downes may have caused people to revise their opinions of Phil.

He returned to action in November at the Seymour Hall in London beating Attu Clottey on points over eight rounds and he ended the year with a points win over Bob Stevens, again over eight rounds at the National Sporting Club.

He got off to a winning start in 1959 with a win on points over Martin Hansen in Cardiff on February 4th though much of the pre-fight publicity centred on Ron "Ponty" Davies who announced his withdrawal from his contest against Pancho Bhatachaji as he felt unable to get his weight down to the contracted poundage.

Later that month, promoter Stan Cottle saw the French Senegalese Michel Diouf knock out Terry Downes in five rounds. This result was regarded as a huge upset and Stan felt that a contest against Diouf would be a good match for Phil at this stage. He urged matchmaker Harry Gorman to go ahead and arrange the contest acknowledging that it would cost serious money to make the match. The contest was set for Sophia Gardens, Cardiff on May 27th while the boxing writers predicted a stern test for Phil and foresaw a rugged battle.

Dave Phillips, writing in the South Wales Echo drew attention to the fact that they had both outpointed Martin Hansen and both had stopped the Frenchman Jacques Barlet but the key form line for Dave was the outcome of their respective contests with Terry Downes and Phillips suggested that this would perhaps be Phil`s sternest test.

To his great credit, Phil emerged as the winner on points over ten rounds and he remained unbeaten through 1959 winning two more ten-rounders in Aberdare and Ebbw Vale. Apart from a no contest against Del Flanagan at Wembley in March, 1960, when referee Tommy Little disqualified both boxers for persistent holding, Phil`s unbeaten run continued and he was eventually granted a return against Terry Downes. The contest took place at Wembley on July 5th, 1960 but this time Phil was stopped in the twelfth round. It was yet another gruelling battle with both Phil and Benny confident that they could win but with Terry Downes not in the mood to surrender his hard-won title. Phil and Terry punched away at each other furiously for twelve rounds but in the end, the pace set by Downes proved to be too much for the Cardiff man, whose face was badly marked when the end came. Phil came close to being floored when he was caught by a right as the bell sounded to end the tenth round but his courage earned the enduring respect and admiration of the "Paddington Express" who himself needed to have some head cuts stitched at St. Mary`s Hospital following the contest.

The records of Phil and Terry reveal a number of common opponents with Edwards getting the better of some of the men who beat Downes but styles make fights and this is what makes the sport of boxing so fascinating and it is fair to say that Terry undoubtedly had Phil`s number.

Following the defeat by Downes, Phil now needed to re-establish himself, but in November he was stopped in four rounds by Orlando Paso at Cheltenham. They met on four occasions with Phil claiming the decision three times over ten rounds so this result was another undoubted setback.

In February 1961 he was nominated to face John "Cowboy" McCormack in a final eliminator for the British Middleweight Title. The contest was staged at Paisley Ice Rink and Phil slipped to his third successive defeat, losing on points over twelve rounds. To his credit, Phil returned to action in Cardiff in June and beat Neal Rivers on points in a ten round contest and he ended the year by stopping Pat O`Grady at Bermondsey in the fifth round.

The year 1962 would prove to be the final year of Phil`s career. He engaged in four ten-rounders and all four went the distance. The first brought him a points win against Liverpool`s Harry Scott, a man who would create his own piece of boxing history by winning and losing against the fearsome Rubin Hurricane Carter and facing the legendary Emile Griffith a year before Emile took the

World Middleweight Title from Dick Tiger in New York.

In May, Phil beat the experienced Orlando Paso at Maesteg and in June he travelled to North Wales to outpoint Billy de Priest at Corwen. Once more the British Boxing Board of Control nominated Phil to box an eliminator for the British Title and this time he was to face George Aldridge at Leicester. In the end, Phil lost the decision and decided to retire from the sport he had graced for a decade.

His record shows a sprinkling of knockouts and stoppage wins but the vast majority of his contests were settled on points giving the fans ample opportunity to appreciate his undoubted skills.

After retiring from the ring Phil assisted Benny in the training of the ever growing number of fighters in his stable and later he took out a manager`s licence himself. He eventually decided to take out a promoter`s licence and provided regular work for members of the stable, notably at the Drill Hall in Dumfries Place. He was a member of the Welsh Area Council and as well as his continued involvement in boxing he was the proprietor of a café in Cardiff for some time, but we should not lose sight of the fact that at his peak, this skilful boxer only lost to the very best.

Phil Edwards

Middleweight
Cardiff
Born: May 12th, 1936

1952

Oct 28	Fred Leek	Willenhall	w.ko.2
Nov 3	Johnny Williamson	Cheltenham	w.rsc.4
Nov 24	Jimmy Ryan	Weston S. Mare	w.ko.2
Dec 1	Gabe Fox	Walsall	w.rsc.5
Dec 10	Paul Hogg	Willenhall	w.ko.1

1953

Jan 5	Frank Guest	Walsall	w.pts.6
Jan 19	Dennis Thomas	Birmingham	w.pts.6
Feb 2	Tom Berry	Walsall	w.pts.6
Feb 16	Ron Atkins	Cardiff	w.pts.6
Feb 24	Johnny Bradford	Willenhall	w.pts.6
Mar 2	Ken Ashwood	Walsall	w.pts.6
Mar 24	Art Henry	Willenhall	w.pts.6
Apr 13	Danny Bonser	Walsall	w.pts.6
May 4	Art Henry	Walsall	w.pts.6
Jun 2	Beau Griffiths	Port Talbot	w.pts.6
Jun 18	Beau Griffiths	Cardiff	w.rsc.3
Jun 29	Danny Doran	Birmingham	w.pts.6
Jul 27	Ray Corbett	Cardiff	w.pts.6
Aug 31	Les Garbett	Birmingham	w.pts.6
Sep 28	Bill Wooding	Birmingham	l.pts.6
Oct 13	Johnny Williamson	Willenhall	w.pts.6
Oct 26	Andy Andrews	Cardiff	w.ko.6
Nov 2	Jim Stimpson	Walsall	l.pts.6

1954

Jan 19	Terry Thompson	Willenhall	w.rsc.5
Feb 23	Bamber Gaye	Willenhall	w.ko.4
Mar 1	Jimmy Brogden	Walsall	d.pts.6
Apr 12	Malcolm Innocent	Cardiff	w.rsc.1
May 1	Jim Stimpson	Newtown	d.pts.6
May 11	Norman Saunders	Earls Court	d.pts.6
May 24	Fred Balio	Cardiff	w.pts.8

1955   *Inactive*

1956

Apr 17	Bob Jeacock	Birmingham	w.rsc.3
May 7	Ken Mullins	Maindy	w.rsc.4
Jul 16	Johnny Williamson	Maindy	w.pts.8
Oct 1	Colin Spittle	Walsall	w.pts.8
Nov 12	Sammy Milsom	Cardiff	w.rsc.6

1957

Jan 16	Noel Trigg	Cardiff	w.pts.8
Mar 5	Jackie Scott	Birmingham	w.rsc.3
Mar 18	Jack Johnson Kofi Cofie	Cardiff	w.pts.8
Mar 29	Gerry McNally	Manchester	w.pts.8
May 17	Eddie Lennon	Belle Vue, Man.	w.rsc.6
May 22	Jack Johnson Kofi Cofie	Streatham	w.rsc.4
Jun 1	Jimmy Lynas	Manchester	w.pts.8
Jul 15	Paddy Delargy	Abergavenny	w.ko.3
Aug 21	Freddie Cross	Cross Keys	w.pts.12
	(Welsh Middleweight Title)		
Sep 9	Dick Tiger	Sophia Gardens	l.pts.10

1958

Jan 28	Lew Lazar	Harringay	w.rsc.5
Feb 11	John Woolard	Birmingham	w.pts.8
Feb 21	Olle Bengtsson	Gothenburg	w.pts.6
Apr 3	Jimmy Lynas	Birmingham	w.pts.8
Apr 23	Freddie Cross	Cardiff	w.pts.12
	(Welsh Middleweight Title)		
Jun 11	Jacques Barlet	London	w.rsc.7
Jul 9	Jean Ruellet	Coney Beach	w.pts.10
Sep 30	Terry Downes	Harringay	l.rsc.13
	(Vacant British Middleweight Title)		
Nov 27	Attu Clottey	Seymour Hall	w.pts.8
Dec 29	Bob Stevens	NSC	w.pts.8

1959

Feb 4	Martin Hansen	Cardiff	w.pts.10
May 27	Michel Diouf	Cardiff	w.pts.10
Jul 14	Remo Carati	Aberdare	w.pts.10
Sep 14	Orlando Paso	Ebbw Vale	w.pts.10

1960

Jan 19	Michel Diouf	Streatham	w.pts.10
Mar 8	Del Flanagan	Wembley	NC 7
Mar 21	Orlando Paso	Derby	w.pts.10
Apr 6	Attu Clottey	Wolverhampton	w.pts.10
Jul 5	Terry Downes	Wembley	l.rsc.12
	(British Middleweight Title)		
Nov 25	Orlando Paso	Cheltenham	l.rsc.4

1961

Feb 22	John (Cowboy) McCormack	Paisley	l.pts.12
	(Final Elim. British Middleweight Title)		
Jun 21	Neal Rivers	Cardiff	w.pts.10
Dec 20	Pat O'Grady	Bermondsey	w.rsc.5

1962

Mar 12	Harry Scott	Manchester	w.pts.10
May 15	Orlando Paso	Maesteg	w.pts.10
Jun 29	Billy de Priest	Corwen	w.pts.10
Sep 24	George Aldridge	Leicester	l.pts.10
	(Elim. British Middleweight Title)		

Phil Edwards

Phil Edwards out on a training run with Joe Erskine
pic: the Royal Oak Collection

Phil Edwards (right) v Freddie Cross
pic: from the Royal Oak Collection

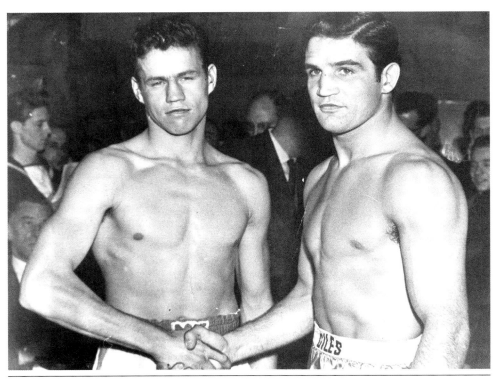

Terry Downes (left) and Phil Edwards weigh-in.
pic: courtesy of Western Mail

Chapter 3

David Hughes, known as "Darkie" to his friends, enjoyed a successful amateur career boxing for Wales and winning the Welsh ABA Welterweight title in 1950 but it was not until 1953 that he turned professional with Benny Jacobs. He made his debut on July 27th and drew over six rounds with Norman Bates. He boxed another five times during the year winning them all, with three of the contests taking place at Willenhall where most of the stable members enjoyed regular work with promoter Alex Griffiths, and two at Walsall.

His winning streak continued into 1954 until he lost on points to Frank Parkes at Willenhall in November. Parkes, a good class fighter would go on to become a highly respected referee following his retirement.

Darkie began 1955 with a win, but on March 10th he was knocked out in three rounds by Alby Tissong at Liverpool Stadium, a venue which acquired the tag of "Graveyard of Champions". His best win during the year came against the experienced Freddie King who was beaten on points over eight rounds at Cardiff's Maindy Stadium on a bill which featured stable-mate Joe Erskine knocking out Baby de Voogd in the first round.

Boswell St. Louis was Darkie's first opponent in 1956 at Walsall Town Hall. The venue is a typical English Town Hall and is ideal for atmospheric small-hall promotions. Darkie lost on points over eight rounds to the Trinidadian, who, in the previous year had been stopped in five rounds by Duilio Loi in Milan, but who would later go on to meet the likes of Peter Waterman, Mick Leahy, Wally Swift and Sammy McSpadden, all champions. He would also face Darkie's stable-mate Tanos Lambrianides but towards the end of his remarkable 99 fight career he was losing more than he was winning.

Following his defeat to Boswell St. Louis, David was back in action at the end of January when he beat Ebe Mensah on points over eight rounds at Carmarthen. Wins followed over Kurt Ernest and Ted Ansell and then on July 16th he was matched with Willie Lloyd at Maindy Stadium for the vacant Welsh Lightweight Title. Darkie lost on points to the Crickhowell man who would also prove to be a thorn in the flesh of Dave Charnley, who went on to dominate the Lightweight division in Britain for about eight years. There were three more contests during the year but he surprisingly lost on points in October to Ebe Mensah at Liverpool.

Darkie kept busy through 1957 boxing on seven occasions. He began with a points win over Paddy Graham in Belfast, where his skills won the appreciation of a partisan crowd and later in the year he beat Jim McCormack. Three more wins followed in 1958 with contests in Belfast, Cardiff and Earls Court but in November he faced the tough French Algerian Guy Gracia, with Cardiff referee Joe Morgan having to rescue Darkie in the tenth and final round.

Gracia had already beaten Dave Charnley at Harringay in November 1955. He went on to beat Joe Lucy, Sammy McCarthy and Willie Lloyd, who was knocked out in their contest at the Empress Hall, Earls Court. In 1958 he stopped South African Willie Toweel in seven rounds at the Kelvin Hall in Glasgow and in March 1959 he would go on to beat Dave Charnley once more, this time on points over ten rounds at Wembley. Gracia finally retired in 1962 following defeats by Maurice Cullen and Johnny Cooke, having notched up 44 wins and 19 losses in a 68 fight career.

Darkie boxed only twice in 1959 but in 1960 he was well and truly in championship contention. In June he beat Londoner Dave Stone on points over ten rounds in an eliminator for the British Lightweight Title. Darkie was a clever, cagey fighter and his skills were often under-rated, so much so, that Dave Stone's fans thought that the more aggressive style of their man would see him through to an easy victory.

After beating Sammy Cowan on a fifth round disqualification Darkie beat Billy Kelly in November in a final eliminator, the match being made over twelve rounds. The contest took place at Sophia Gardens and the bill also featured stablemate Terry Crimmins who faced the tough Scot Tommy Burgoyne in what was a memorable contest.

At 29, Darkie had boxed professionally for seven years when he was granted this final eliminator. As always, he did nearly all the leading with his left hand and when the counterpunches came from Kelly he would get inside and prevent the Irishman from landing his heavier punches.

The solid blows came from Kelly but Darkie used his speed about the ring and referee Tommy Little raised his hand without hesitation at the final bell, though it had not been an easy contest. Kelly was always dangerous, but Darkie had never trained harder and was not going to be denied on this occasion.

The stage was now set for his British title challenge against Dave Charnley, but unbelievably, Darkie had been inactive for a year when his chance came. His contest with Charnley was set for November 20th, 1961 at Nottingham Ice Rink with British, Empire and European titles at stake. Darkie was set to receive a career-best purse of £800 while Charnley, who had not been called upon to defend his British title in over four years was due to receive just over £2,000.

Darkie was a quiet, genial character but had become rather bitter regarding his boxing career. Manager Benny Jacobs had always found difficulty in obtaining contests for him and Benny claimed that managers ran for cover when Darkie's name was mentioned as an opponent for their fighters, but both Benny and Darkie felt that one day the title fight would come and they never gave up hope.

There is no question that they were unlucky in coming up against Charnley, a man who won his British title against Joe Lucy, his Empire crown from Willie Toweel and his European championship from Mario Vecchiatto. He had also challenged the legendary Joe "Old Bones" Brown for the world title. In their first meeting at Houston, Dave sustained a badly cut eye and had to retire after eight rounds, but in the rematch in London, Charnley took Brown right down to the wire before losing on points after making a huge effort in the later rounds.

This was the calibre of the champion facing Darkie across the ring at Nottingham and sadly, he was knocked out in the first round. Benny, with his characteristic humour, insisted in his post-fight interviews that his man was ahead at the time!

Alan Wood, writing in the Western Mail described the contest as follows: "Charnley went for Hughes from the first bell. He had him staggering against the ropes and Hughes went down for a count of three before staggering to his feet. Then Charnley went after him like a tiger.

He got Hughes in his own corner, clipped him with a right hand to the side of the head, and then landed a terrific left hook to the jaw.

Hughes went down like "a sack of coal" and his head struck the canvas.

He was completely unconscious and he remained there for at least two minutes after the count while a doctor was called.

The gumshield was removed from his mouth and he had to be given as much fresh air as possible, with the towel and ice packs placed around his neck.

Hughes was still in a dazed state when he left the ring and quite obviously did not know what was happening and had not recovered his reflexes".

Charnley had not expected the contest to end so quickly but saw his opportunity and took it, while Benny expressed the view that Charnley was the best lightweight in the world.

Clearly "Father Time" and a lengthy lay-off could not be beaten, especially bearing in mind the power of Charnley and his standing in world terms. In reality, this was a devastating defeat and recovery would take some time. Darkie returned to the ring at Carmarthen in June 1963 with a points win over Tommy Atkins but he was then inactive until May 1964 when he was beaten on points over six rounds at Solihull by Yvon John Jarret and this turned out to be his final contest. Topping the bill was Johnny Prescott against the Spanish Heavyweight Champion, Benito Canal with the Birmingham man taking a close verdict on points after ten rounds. David, weighing in at 10st 7lbs contributed to what Boxing News described as an "entertaining six-rounder", and sadly , coming at the end of his career these words do not reflect the skills which he brought to the ring throughout his career.

David "Darkie" Hughes eventually became a member of the Welsh Area Council of the British Boxing Board of Control and he served as an inspector for many years. He always went about his work quietly but his dry sense of humour was never very far below the surface.

David 'Darkie' Hughes

Lightweight
Cardiff
Born: April 10, 1931
Welsh ABA Welterweight Champion, 1950

1953

Jul 27	Norman Bates	Cardiff	d.6
Oct 13	Emrys Jones	Willenhall	w.pts.6
Oct 26	Norman Bates	Cardiff	w.ko.4
Nov 2	Maurice Williams	Walsall	w.pts.6
Nov 17	Stuart Finch	Willenhall	w.ko.3
Dec 15	Jeff Walters	Willenhall	w.pts.8

1954

Mar 1	Harold Palmer	Walsall	w.ko.3
Apr 5	Jim Stimpson	Walsall	w.pts.8
May 1	Johnny Ritchie	Newtown	w.rsc.5
Jul 19	Derek Davis	Cardiff	w.rsc.2
Oct 11	Bill Sliney	Haverfordwest	w.ko.1
Oct 26	Del Willis	Walsall	w.rsc.4
Nov 30	Frank Parkes	Willenhall	l.pts.8

1955

Feb 7	Bola Lawal	Walsall	w.pts.8
Mar 10	Alby Tissong	Liverpool	l.ko.3
May 16	Johnny Miller	Birmingham	l.dis. 6
Jun 9	Jimmy McLachlan	Birmingham	w.pts.8
Jul 18	Freddie King	Maindy Stadium	w.pts.8
Nov 28	Ray Corbett	Malvern	l.pts.8

1956

Jan 2	Boswell St. Louis	Walsall	l.pts.8
Jan 30	Ebe Mensah	Carmarthen	w.pts.8
Mar 5	Kurt Ernest	Birmingham	w.pts.8
May 16	Ted Ansell	Hereford	w.rsc.7
Jul 16	Willie Lloyd	Maindy Stadium	l.pts.12
	(Vacant Welsh Lightweight Title)		
Aug 23	Syd Greb	Liverpool	w.pts.8
Oct 11	Ebe Mensah	Liverpool	l.pts.8
Nov 12	George Whelan	Cardiff	w.pts.8

1957

Jan 19	Paddy Graham	Belfast	w.pts.10
Mar 29	John McNally	Manchester	d.8
May 7	Paddy Graham	London	l.ko.3
May 17	Kurt Ernest	Manchester	w.rtd.5
Aug 21	Arty Magill	Cross Keys	w.rsc.2
Oct 21	Jim McCormack	Cardiff	w.pts.8
Dec 2	Andy Baird	Cheltenham	w.pts.8

1958

Mar 8	Jimmy Brown	Belfast	w.pts.8
Apr 23	Andy Baird	Cardiff	w.pts.8
May 20	George Martin	Earls Court	w.pts.8
Nov 12	Guy Gracia	Cardiff	l.rsc.10

1959

Feb 17	Eddie Hughes	London	w.pts.8
Apr 15	Eddie Hughes	Cardiff	w.pts.8

1960

Jun 7	Dave Stone	London	w.pts.10
	(Elim. British Lightweight Title)		
Sep 22	Sammy Cowan	Cardiff	w.dis.5
Nov 24	Billy Kelly	Cardiff	w.pts.12
	(Final Elim. British Lightweight Title)		

1961

Nov 20	Dave Charnley	Nottingham	l.ko.1
	(British, Empire and European Lightweight Title)		

1963

Jun 24	Tommy Atkins	Carmarthen	w.pts.8

1964

May 6	Yvon John Jarret	Solihull	l.pts.6

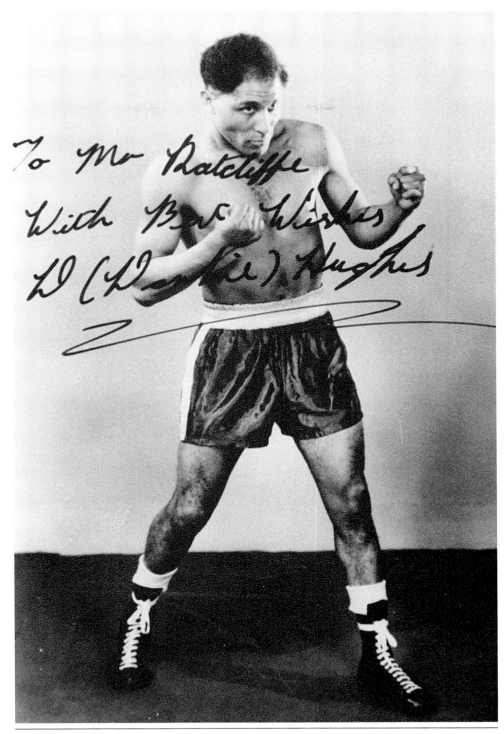

To Mr Ratcliffe
With Best Wishes
D (Darkie) Hughes

David 'Darkie' Hughes

Chapter 4

Teddy Best made his professional debut at Coney Beach Arena, Porthcawl on August 26th, 1953 and in the next ten years engaged in sixtyone contests. He recorded twentyseven wins, thirtyone losses and three draws, statistics which hardly do justice to an uncompromising fighter who just did not know the meaning of taking it easy in the gym.

He was a busy fighter and after beating Ray Smith on points over six rounds in his first contest, he notched up another seven contests before the end of the year. He lost just once, being stopped in the third round by Parry Dando, an opponent he would face twice more in future contests.

He boxed nine times during 1954, frequently appearing on shows in the Midlands and on May 1st he faced Emrys Jones at Newtown in an eliminator for the Welsh Lightweight Title. Teddy was disqualified in the eighth round and would have to wait more than three years for his shot at the crown. His next contest was at Wembley Town Hall when he lost on points to Charlie Page and after stopping Bill Sliney he faced Parry Dando once more, this time losing on points. He rounded off the year by beating Bryn Phillips on points over eight rounds at Carmarthen and then stopped Roy Coles in the fifth round at Walsall Town Hall.

He had seven contests in 1955 with mixed results and on July 26th, he was matched with Dave Charnley at Birmingham. Teddy lost on points over eight rounds in what was Charnley`s twelfth contest. Charnley was undefeated, the sole blemish on his record being a draw against Welshman Willie Lloyd who would later go on to register a win over the "Dartford Destroyer".

The contest against Charnley was a tough one but Teddy put up a fine display against one of the finest young lightweights in the country. Best was puzzled by Charnley`s southpaw stance for a time and his best work was at close-quarters. Charnley picked his punches well and was the cleaner hitter. Teddy was cut over the left eye in the sixth round and was floored for a count of eight by a sharp right to the chin.

The exchanges during the last round were hectic and both boxers fell to the floor following a tussle on the ropes but Charnley had done enough to secure the decision.

In May, 1956 Teddy was matched with Willie Lloyd at Maindy Stadium and held the experienced Crickhowell man to a draw over eight rounds. Topping the bill was the contest between Joe Erskine and Dick Richardson, with Joe taking the decision on points over ten rounds. This contest followed appearances at

Harringay and Earls Court, and a week after the Lloyd contest he was stopped in seven rounds by Johnny Miller at West Hartlepool. In October, he met Parry Dando for the third time, on this occasion at Abergavenny, and this time he stopped Dando in the fifth round.

To round off the year he lost on points over eight rounds to Ebe Mensah in Cardiff. Mensah himself was looked after by Benny for part of his career and in 1957 Teddy beat Bryn Phillips in the second of their three fight series. He beat Barney Beale in the first contest of yet another three fight series and then came a revenge win over George Whelan who was stopped in the first round.

In August, 1957 Teddy, after a long wait, finally got his opportunity to challenge for the Welsh Lightweight title and he stopped Bryn Phillips, from Fishguard in the ninth round of their battle at Cross Keys. Topping the bill was Phil Edwards against Freddie Cross in their Welsh title tussle. Teddy had first been earmarked to challenge Willie Lloyd for the championship only to be thwarted by the decision of the Crickhowell man to retire from boxing but he finally achieved his ambition of winning the Welsh Lightweight title with four of his stablemates on the bill and with all of them successful.

At the weigh-in Phillips scaled 9st.8.1/2 lbs with Best coming in just four ounces heavier.

Teddy stormed into Bryn Phillips from the first bell and handed out some heavy punishment. He attacked fiercely and flattened Phillips with a hard right hook and bludgeoned his opponent to the canvas again in the second round for another count of eight.

In the third round, Best flailed away in windmill style and Bryn went down for a count of nine from a hard right cross. He then landed a tremendous right to the body which floored the battered Phillips for another count of nine.

They fought toe to toe for the next six rounds with Phillips giving as good as he got, but he was limping and obviously in great pain. Before the bell sounded for the beginning of the tenth round Phillips indicated his retirement and promptly announced his retirement from boxing. Little did Teddy realise in the joy of victory that it would be six years before he would be called upon to defend his title and sadly, after winning the title he would only register six wins in the remaining twentythree contests of his career, but he was still good enough to offer stern tests to several of the up and coming boxers in the lightweight division.

In April, 1958 he stopped Con Mount Bassie, sparring partner to Willie Toweel, flooring his opponent four times in the first round before referee D.S.Davies intervened after just two minutes of action, and in November, he lost on points to Jimmy Brown over in Belfast while in October, 1959 he beat the highly regarded Dennis Hinson. In February, 1960 he went over to Dublin and stopped Billy "Spider" Kelly in the fourth round. Kelly had previously held the British and Empire Featherweight titles and had faced the likes of Hogan Bassey, Ray Famechon, Willie Toweel and Ronnie Clayton, though by now he was nearing the end of his career. In April, Teddy went over to Cherbourg and lost on points over ten rounds to Manuel Sosa. Later in the year he faced Dave Coventry and Dave Stone at Liverpool Stadium and Streatham Ice Rink respectively at a time when both were highly regarded at the lightweight poundage and he ended the year travelling to Rome, where he was stopped in eight rounds by Luigi Castoldi.

He was inactive during 1961 and boxed just twice in 1962. In August, 1963 he was held to a draw by Gordon Davies in a contest for the Welsh Lightweight title and Teddy finally decided to retire later that month after he was stopped by Peter Cheevers in the first round at the Majestic Ballroom, Finsbury Park.

The contest against Gordon Davies took place at Newtown and topping the bill was Joe Erskine against the American, Freddie Mack which saw Joe winning on points over ten rounds while Dennis Pleace, Geoff Rees and Ron Lendrum also appeared on the bill and each registered a win. Lendrum was described in the South Wales Echo as being the most impressive winner on the bill and looked set for a rapid rise up the ladder of success. Brian Madley wrote: "He is a brilliant boxer in the classical style and proved that he also packs a punch by stopping Enfield's Dave Johnson in the fourth round".

As is often the case Teddy Best and Gordon Davies served up a contest worthy of the Welsh title. When two fighters are evenly matched a cracking contest frequently results and there have been so many Welsh title fights that fall into this category.

Brian Madley wrote: "Best retained his title by holding Davies to a draw – or perhaps it would be more accurate to say that Davies held the champion to a draw for it was the veteran Cardiff boxer who made all the early running.

Davies looked nervous at the start and was troubled by Best's hooks in the third.

But he recovered well to get his left jab working and proceeded to close the points gap until at the end of ten rounds the referee decided that he had done enough to share the verdict".

Within a month, Teddy had made his final appearance, but the ferocity of his work in the ring still lives on in the minds of his former stablemates and even as a senior citizen his shoulders still have that look of power.

Teddy Best

Lightweight
Cardiff
Born: September 24th, 1933
Welsh Lightweight Champion

1953

Aug 26	Ray Smith	Coney Beach	w.pts.6
Aug 31	Andy Baird	Birmingham	l.pts.4
Sep 28	Tom Berry	Birmingham	w.ko.3
Oct 13	Dennis Cotton	Willenhall	w.ko.1
Oct 26	Parry Dando	Cardiff	l.rsc.3
Dec 7	Ray Corbett	Walsall	w.pts.6
Dec 15	Mike Hughes	Willenhall	w.pts.6
Dec 28	Vic Glover	Birmingham	w.pts.8

1954

Jan 19	Emrys Jones	Willenhall	d.pts.8
Jan 25	Harold Palmer	Birmingham	w.pts.8
Feb 23	Maurice Williams	Willenhall	w.ko.3
May 1	Emrys Jones	Newtown	l.dis.8
	(Final Elim. Welsh Lightweight Title)		
Jun 15	Charlie Page	Wembley Town Hall	l.pts.8
Jul 19	Bill Sliney	Cardiff	w.rsc.4
Oct 4	Parry Dando	Cardiff	l.pts.8
Oct 25	Bryn Phillips	Carmarthen	w.pts.8
Dec 7	Roy Coles	Walsall	w.rsc.5

1955

Jan 3	Bola Lawal	Walsall	l.pts.8
Apr 18	Ray Corbett	Birmingham	l.pts.8
Jul 26	Dave Charnley	Birmingham	l.pts.8
Aug 29	Cyril Evans	Maindy Stadium	w.ko.1
Sep 26	Benny Kid Chocolate	Carmarthen	w.pts.8
Oct 10	Pat McCoy	Cardiff	l.pts.8
Dec 13	Johnny Mann	Birmingham	l.pts.8

1956

Jan 16	Pat McCoy	Cardiff	w.pts.8
Jan 31	Dennis Hinson	West Ham	l.pts.8
Feb 7	Leo Molloy	Harringay	w.pts.6
Mar 20	George Whelan	Earls Court	l.pts.8
May 7	Willie Lloyd	Maindy	d.pts.8
May 14	Johnny Miller	West Hartlepool	l.rsc.7
Oct 29	Parry Dando	Abergavenny	w.rsc.5
Nov 12	Ebe Mensah	Cardiff	l.pts.8

1957

Jan 16	Bryn Phillips	Cardiff	w.pts.8
Mar 18	Barney Beale	Cardiff	w.pts.6
May 7	George Whelan	London	w.rsc.1
May 27	Arthur Murphy	Cardiff	w.rsc.6
Jun 18	George Martin	London	l.pts.8
Aug 21	Bryn Phillips	Cross Keys	w.rtd.9
	(Welsh Lightweight Title)		
Sep 9	John McNally	Cardiff	l.dis.7

1958

Apr 23	Con Mount Bassie	Cardiff	w.rsc.1
May 17	Andy Baird	Newtown	w.pts.8
Sep 22	Eddie Hughes	Abergavenny	l.pts.8
Oct 6	Ray Ashie	Maesteg	l.pts.8
Nov 29	Jimmy Brown	Belfast	l.pts.8

1959

Jan 20	Barney Beale	London	l.pts.8
Aug 22	Tommy McGuiness	Colwyn Bay	w.rsc.3
Oct 28	Dennis Hinson	Cardiff	w.pts.8
Dec 8	Barney Beale	London	l.pts.8

1960

Feb 8	Brian Jones	Derby	l.pts.10
Feb 18	Billy Kelly	Dublin	w.rsc.4
Mar 21	Brian Jones	Derby	l.pts.8
Apr 9	Manuel Sosa	Cherbourg	l.pts.10
Apr 25	Brian Jones	Nottingham	l.pts.8
May 5	Dave Covent	Liverpool	l.pts.8
Aug 30	Dave Stone	London	l.pts.8
Nov 25	Luigi Castoldi	Rome	l.rtd.8

1961   *Inactive*

1962

Sep 26	Billy Elliott	Solihull	w.rsc.1
Nov 28	Chris Elliott	Solihull	l.pts.8

1963

Mar 12	Brian Jones	Birmingham	l.rtd.5
Aug 10	Gordon Davies	Newtown	d.10
	(Welsh Lightweight Title)		
Aug 27	Peter Cheevers	London	l.rsc.1

Teddy Best

Chapter 5

Joe Erskine was born in Angelina Street, Cardiff on January 26th, 1934, a street in the docks area of the city also known as Tiger Bay. His birthplace was just a few hundred yards from that of "Peerless" Jim Driscoll. Also born in the same street was Billy Boston, who would go on to become one of Britain`s finest rugby league stars and as young men they both played in the same local rugby team. Joe was brought up in this fascinating multiracial community which not only produced a galaxy of sports stars but also a number of superb jazz musicians and the internationally famous singing star, Shirley Bassey.

Joe`s father, John, was a Jamaican and his mother was Welsh. John was determined from the start that Joe would be a champion boxer and his grandmother "Nana" became one of Joe`s staunchest supporters as soon as he was drawn to the ring.

As a young boy Joe enjoyed swimming and cricket as well as rugby but began to box at the age of eleven when his father took him to the Victoria Park Amateur Boxing Club and he won a clutch of titles between six and a half and ten stone. He then progressed to Cadet boxing and in 1951 captained the successful Army team at Wembley. In 1952 he became Welsh ABA Lightheavyweight Champion and in 1953 he took the ABA Heavyweight Championship with Henry Cooper retaining his title at Lightheavyweight.

The names of Cooper and Erskine were to be linked throughout their careers in both the amateur and professional codes and in 1953 they were both members of an ABA squad which went to Germany and Italy with Harry Gibbs as the trainer. Gibbs would later go on to become one of Britain`s finest referees in a career spanning twentyfive years while the squad also included Dave Charnley, Frankie Jones and Ron Barton, all future champions.

Joe Erskine turned professional in 1954 with Benny Jacobs and made his professional debut at Hanley less than two months after his twentieth birthday while still in the Army. There was a good deal of support for Joe in the hall as he destroyed Alf Price in less than two rounds, but celebrations were shortlived as he was due back on guard duty at midnight at Nesscliffe Army Camp, Shrewsbury. He notched up fifteen contests in his first year with three of these taking place on the same night when Joe took part in a Novices` Heavyweight Competition arranged by promoter Jack Solomons and his record was perfect save for a draw over six rounds in Cardiff with Dinny Powell.

Joe maintained his momentum through 1955 beating Peter Bates in Birmingham in March and in his eleventh fight of the year he beat Henry

Cooper on points over ten rounds in London on November 15th in a contest which was an eliminator for the British Heavyweight title. Towards the end of the year he was named Best Young Boxer of 1955 by the Boxing Writers Club, an honour which has meant so much to many of our boxers over the years because it comes from within the sport.

In May, 1956 he beat fellow Welshman Dick Richardson on points over ten rounds in Cardiff. Dick, known as the "Maesglas Marciano" was a tough battler in the ring and Joe was soon in trouble. A cut which Joe had sustained in training reopened almost immediately and in the fifth round Joe went to the canvas for the first time in his career, but from that point onwards he showed the qualities of a champion and got up off the floor to take a well deserved points decision.

Johnny Lewis, trainer of Dick Richardson tells how Joe earned just £2,000 for this contest, with Dick taking considerably more, but Benny soon realised the value of his fighters and they all earned well with him.

Cuts were to remain a huge problem for Joe but after this injury had healed, his big chance came. Joe was still undefeated when he was matched with Johnny Williams at Maindy Stadium in Cardiff on August 27th for the Heavyweight Championship of Great Britain. This was the first time that two Welshmen had met for the heavyweight crown and Joe became the fourth Welshman to win the title following in the footsteps of Jack Petersen, Tommy Farr and Johnny Williams, who had taken the title from Jack Gardner in 1952. Johnny lost the title to Don Cockell in 1953 and the championship was now vacant following Cockell`s retirement. The contest against Williams proved to be a hard battle and once more Joe was to be handicapped by cuts, this time over both eyes. He had to dig deep and survived some desperate moments before emerging with the points decision over fifteen rounds. The Lonsdale Belt was fastened around his waist and torrential rain greeted the new champion.

On February 19th, 1957 Joe was matched with the tough Cuban, Nino Valdes. Valdes proved more than a match for British heavyweights forcing Don Cockell into third round retirement, though to his credit, Dick Richardson lasted into the eighth round at Harringay, by which time he had picked up eye injuries which were serious enough to bring about the intervention of the referee.

Valdes totally overwhelmed Joe, knocking him out in the first round and giving him his first taste of defeat but some of his former stablemates remain convinced that on this occasion Joe was a beaten man before he stepped into the ring. Both Valdes and his manager Bobby Gleason were ecstatic after the contest. Nino had warmed up with about half an hour of shadow boxing before the fight and Gleason confirmed that the plan was to win quickly. One of the first visitors to his dressing room after the fight was the Cuban Ambassador, Roberto Mendoza, who gave Valdes a congratulatory hug while Nino explained in near disbelief that it had only taken two punches.

Valdes and Gleason were so impressed by their treatment in London they suggested to promoter Jack Solomons that they would like to challenge Floyd Patterson for the world title in London, though as always, Jack had been hoping to push the claims of the home fighter. Valdes had boxed Archie Moore in Las Vegas and felt that he had been robbed. This led him to believe that "the mob" would never let him get near the world title and that Britain provided him with the best opportunity of a level playing field.

For "Jolting Joe", recovery from this setback was of the utmost importance and he went on to beat Peter Bates once again, this time on points over twelve rounds at Doncaster at the end of May. His next contest came on September 17th when he retained his British title against Henry Cooper at London's Harringay Arena. Joe then beat Joe Bygraves for the Empire title with the fight taking place at Nottingham, the Welshman taking the decision on points over fifteen rounds, while for Cooper it had been a miserable year, losing to Bygraves, Ingemar Johannson and ofcourse, Erskine.

Quite naturally, Joe now set his sights on the European title which was held by Sweden's Ingemar Johannson. On February 21st, 1958 the pair met at Gothenburg and Joe was retired by his corner after thirteen rounds. Yet again, Joe was troubled by cuts and took heavy punishment from the big hitting Swede. Ingemar went on to win the world title from Floyd Patterson but lost the next two contests in their three fight series.

In June, 1959 Joe lost his British and Empire titles to Brian London of Blackpool. He was boxing well until the familiar handicap reared its ugly head. Once Joe's left eyebrow had been opened, London fought like a man possessed and ripped the titles away from Erskine, knocking him out in the eighth round. Victory would have given Joe outright ownership of the Lonsdale Belt, but alas, it was not to be.

The turning point in Joe's career undoubtedly came following a decision to have plastic surgery carried out on his eyebrows. After this, life was somewhat easier for Joe in the ring. He came back with a win over Max Brianto in Cardiff and then, in February, 1959 he recorded the finest victory of his career.

On the night when Howard Winstone made his professional debut at Wembley, Joe was matched with the highly regarded American, Willie Pastrano. Willie was fast and skilful and was considered to be one of the finest boxers in the world. He later confirmed this by going on to win the Lightheavyweight Championship of the World. It is some measure of Joe's ability that he was able to outbox a man of Pastrano's calibre. Joe was a clear points winner, moving in to the American at every opportunity and proving to be his master with speedy counterpunching.

Following the contest the American commented: "You sports writers sadly underestimate Erskine. He is undoubtedly the best you have and is a difficult man to beat."

Erskine took the initiative from the first bell connecting with his left and pushing Pastrano to the ropes with a right to the body and he continued to chase the American in the second round. Pastrano began to force the next session but was caught by a right hook to the body and both men punched away at each other.

In the fourth round Erskine was scoring with lefts and both boxers were moving quickly around the ring, while in the next round Pastrano was stalking his man almost like a matador. Through the sixth round Joe displayed some good work inside while Pastrano took the seventh with a constant stream of lefts and showing superb defensive work in the process.

The eighth round was another good one for Pastrano while in the ninth,

Erskine used his left to good effect but with the American scoring with impeccable counterpunching. Joe was at his best as they came out for the last round, beating Pastrano to the punch with superb left hands while slipping many of Willie`s jabs and when the final bell sounded Joe was a deserving winner of this battle of the purists.

Angelo Dundee, Pastrano`s manager was extremely impressed by Joe Erskine. He was surprised by Erskine`s skill and felt that if Joe had been bigger and if he could have developed a heavier punch, he would have been a world beater. This assessment of Joe comes from Dundee`s book, "I Only Talk Winning".

Willie Pastrano had beaten Dick Richardson on points in London in October, 1957. He had also beaten Brian London but lost their return fight on a controversial cut eye stoppage, but following his defeat by Joe, Angelo Dundee decided that Willie`s future should be at lightheavyweight and this turned out to be the perfect solution with Pastrano finally becoming world champion.

Following his win over Pastrano, Joe was once again matched with Dick Richardson, this time at Coney Beach Arena, Porthcawl. Dick was no stranger to the arena having beaten Hans Kalbfell and Bob Baker there and losing to Henry Cooper in the fifth round of his title challenge. Cooper was bleeding badly and was floored in the fifth round in a neutral corner, but Dick, roared on by the crowd, went all out for victory and was floored by a sucker punch. For this contest, Joe weighed in at thirteen stone eight and a half pounds and Dick came in at fourteen stone six and three quarter pounds but in spite of Richardson`s weight advantage, Erskine came through the ten rounds winning on points.

After beating southpaw Bruno Scarabellin on points over ten rounds in August, when Joe did not look particularly good, another meeting with Henry Cooper was put in place with Harry Levene as the promoter and Mickey Duff as matchmaker. Cooper had taken Joe`s British and Empire heavyweight titles from Brian London, and having himself gone through a difficult patch, Henry would now go on to bring stability to the British heavyweight scene and go on to become the longest reigning British Heavyweight Champion.

Over the next few years, Cooper and Erskine met in no less than three title fights with Henry now gaining the upper hand. On November 17th, 1959 Joe was stopped in twelve rounds at London`s Earls Court Arena and in March, 1961 Joe retired in the fifth round with badly cut eyes bringing the contest to an end. Their final meeting came in April, 1962, and once more Joe`s eyes let him down with the contest ending in the ninth round.

It was the contest at Earls Court which left the lasting impression on my mind. Joe was floored by a series of punches which left his body arched over the bottom rope with his head resting on the ring apron, out, to the world. There were some worrying moments and Henry feared the worst, but thankfully, Joe recovered.

During the latter stages of his career, Joe beat George Chuvalo on a fifth round disqualification in Toronto. George was a tough fighter who would later go the full fifteen rounds with both Ernie Terrell and Muhammad Ali in contests for the Heavyweight Championship of the World. Joe also beat the American, Freddie Mack at Newtown, Mid-Wales, but lost to Karl Mildenberger on points over ten rounds in Dortmund.

Joe sustained an eye injury in his contest against the accomplished Mack but in the words of Brian Madley, writing in the South Wales Echo proved "that he is still the fastest heavyweight around but few opponents since Willie Pastrano have made Joe keep up such a hot pace as this man Mack did.

The fight had been underway for only a minute when the notoriously slow-starting Cardiff man was caught by a looping right hand that sent him staggering against the ropes.

But few men have had the honour of putting Joe on the canvas and Mack was soon to find out why. He was never again able to get through with that destructive right although he staged an all-out assault in the ninth round, which once more had Joe defending desperately.

But in the rounds between these moments of Mack supremacy it was the left hand of Erskine that dominated the proceedings.

Afterwards Mack, in his usual best voluble form, said he thought he had done enough to earn a draw and would like a return.

But Erskine, having clearly got over the hurdle will now want to look for new conquests in order to keep up his title challenge".

In 1964, he kept himself in title contention beating both Jack Bodell and Johnny Prescott, but after losing to the "Blond Bomber" Billy Walker on points at Wembley, Joe announced his retirement. Bodell went on to hold the British title briefly and Walker and Prescott will always be remembered for their two epic battles, though significantly, neither won the British title.

Even in the twilight of his career Joe was capable of extending the best of our heavyweights on the domestic front and Joe must have been satisfied with the headline in "Boxing News" after his win over Prescott. The headline ran: "Erskine Gives Prescott Lesson" and the report ran as follows: "Tiger Bay`s Joe Erskine (13-13) had his compatriots singing as the 30-year-old ex-heavyweight champion dished out a thorough 10-round boxing lesson to an aggressive but comparatively inexperienced Johnny Prescott, Birmingham (13-10).

Prescott never looked like justifying unofficial ringside odds of 6-4 on. Erskine simply beat his man on points with the kind of boxing skill for which he is renowned.

Both men sustained eye injuries but there was no question of referee Mickey Fox intervening and it was a mere formality that he had to tot up his card at all.

Erskine missed wildly with two right crosses in the first round but Prescott could not take advantage of the Welshman`s early inaccuracy. They set a hot pace and though Erskine was unable to impress his left hand on proceedings, he stopped the Brummie from getting through with most of his two-handed hooking to the body.

Erskine`s ring work in the second was a treat. He jabbed, feinted and even when Prescott caught him on the ropes later in the round, the Welshman was never in trouble. Some of his moves were vintage Erskine and Prescott finished the round wondering how he could tag the elusive Welshman.

But at the end of the third round Erskine went back to his corner with a slight cut on the left eyebrow. Nevertheless, he took the round with much the same pattern of superb defence and smart jabbings. But some of those Prescott right-crosses had got through, and Erskine, with a minor mark on the right eye as well, had plenty to think about.

The crowd roared when Prescott launched a full-blooded assault at the start of the fourth but hardly a punch touched the will o` the wisp Welshman, who countered crisply to the head. The eye damage looked no worse.

Prescott looked almost desperate as he came out for the fifth. And no wonder! Erskine had his measure now and rattled out the drum beats on the Midlander`s face. Halfway through the round Erskine`s right hand opened a cut over Prescott`s left eye and the Brummie was in real trouble when Erskine met him with a solid right to the chin.

Prescott, for all his gameness and strength, just could not hurt the Welshman. Erskine rode the punches, absorbed them on his arms and all the time maintained a tremendous barrage of scoring points.

The saturation effect of all the blows Erskine had landed had a marked effect in the seventh. Prescott was bleeding from the left eyebrow but there was also blood seeping from Erskine`s vulnerable left eyebrow.

Surprisingly Erskine was the livelier boxer in the last three rounds and he continued to beat home a painful lesson. The home crowd applauded Erskine as he jolted Prescott`s head with solid lefts and tied him up as he tried to come close.

In the ninth another cut opened further along Erskine`s eyebrow and Prescott, sensing this as his only chance of victory, forged forward. Then for the only time Erskine appeared a little perturbed".

Following the victory over Prescott, there was a great deal of interest in a meeting with Billy Walker. Opinion was sharply divided over the outcome, with George Walker, brother-manager of Billy, stating that they would stop Joe by the halfway mark, but both Benny and Joe were supremely confident. In a pre-fight interview, Joe said: "Johnny Prescott clearly outpointed Walker and you know how easily I dealt with Johnny." Joe badly needed the money at this point in time and desperately wanted to win a Lonsdale Belt outright. He felt sure he would succeed and stated that should he lose the contest he would retire.

Boxing News predicted that Erskine would beat Walker barring eye injuries and they foresaw a battle between the veteran`s skill and speed of hand and foot against the youngster`s explosive power and sheer brute strength, but history shows that Walker was given the decision on points over ten rounds and a disillusioned Joe did indeed retire from the sport he had graced for so long.

Joe trained extremely hard for the contest and came in at 13st. 12lbs with Walker coming in 2.1/2 lbs heavier. Joe boxed well up to the end of the seventh round and at this point he was arguably ahead. Walker then realised that he would need to pull out all the stops against the old boxing master and it was from this point onwards that the strength of Walker became the telling factor. The West Ham fighter never looked like knocking Joe out but he had the power in his legs and the determination to go forward.

Walker went for a grandstand finish throwing everything he could at Erskine during those final three minutes and Joe seemed only too glad to hang on. Billy virtually ignored Joe`s left hand throughout the contest as he bulldozed forward intent on crushing the Welshman and was warned a few times for butting by referee Tommy Little and after the contest Benny Jacobs insisted that he would complain to the British Boxing Board of Control about the handling of the contest. Benny was convinced that Joe had been butted or hit low on at least thirty occasions.

Joe, on the other hand, expressed the view that he had done enough to win, though he acknowledged that he ran out of steam during the last three rounds while Billy Walker insisted that he had boxed to orders, pacing the contest, and putting Joe under pressure in the last three rounds.

In truth, Joe knew what he had to do, but towards the end of the contest he lacked the strength to deal adequately with his younger opponent. The defeat hurt, and this turned out to be Joe`s farewell to the ring.

In a ten year professional career Joe met many of the big names in the heavyweight division both at domestic and world level and could look back on his record with pride. He did not enjoy roadwork and did not enjoy going backwards in the ring, but he was at his best going forward and countering. His skills were exquisite but the paper thin skin around his eyes proved to be a major problem and I feel sure that had Joe been a bigger man he would have been a serious threat at world level because almost all of his defeats came at the hands of big punchers.

From a personal point of view, I shall always remember Joe as a very quiet, gentle person who accepted the cards dealt to him with dignity. Life was not too kind to him after retirement and the money soon disappeared, some say because of his liking for a bet. As a youngster, dice was a popular pastime on the streets of the "Bay" and one of his friends was even shot during a game, while Joe`s passion for gambling led to the loss of £2,000 on the night of his contest with Johansson in Sweden. His health began to deteriorate as a result of sickle cell anaemia, but he always remained friends with his old manager Benny Jacobs, and when Benny got to the stage where he was confined to a wheelchair, Joe would always bring Benny to the ringside on fight night. It was a touching sight though I doubt that either would have wanted sympathy!

Throughout his life, Joe remained close to his roots and in retirement he was a creature of habit. Each day, he would emerge from his house immaculately dressed in a suit and would stroll down to Bab`s Bistro in Tiger Bay. This allowed Joe to have his first pint of the day before official licensing hours clicked in. Later he would visit his favourite pubs such as "The Packet" and would end up at the "Royal Oak", the pub which for many years was associated with the Driscoll family. Here, Joe would round off the night, occupying a stool in the corner of a room known as the "office" and when the bell sounded at closing time, his friend Jackie Chambers, himself a boxing trainer, would jokingly warn customers to keep out of Joe`s way, but in truth, he was the most genial of souls.

Early in 1990, Joe Erskine succumbed to illness at the age of 56 and on a cold February day, his funeral service was held at the church of St Mary the Virgin on Bute Street. The church was packed with personalities from the world of sport and there were many local people present. On his arrival at the church, Jack Petersen was asked if he would speak and paid handsome tribute to Joe while, earlier that morning, he himself had been diagnosed as suffering from cancer. As well as the tributes, local people sang as the community paid homage to one of its own.

Even though much of the "Bay" was now being redeveloped, Joe`s coffin was carried through the streets, and in scenes which were reminiscent of the passing of Jim Driscoll, the headline in the South Wales Echo read: "As Great a Grief as Peerless Jim", and this surely reflects the way in which Joe Erskine, a local hero, had touched the lives of so many people. The love, affection and support of his community, for Joe, was the ultimate crown.

Joe Erskine

Heavyweight
Cardiff
Born: January 26th, 1934
Welsh ABA Lightheavyweight Champion, 1952
ABA Heavyweight Champion, 1953

1954

Mar 9	Alf Price	Hanley	w.ko.2
Mar 16	Tom Rodgers	Willenhall	w.rsc.2
Mar 22	Frank Walker	Birmingham	w.dis.5
Apr 12	Dinny Powell	Cardiff	d.pts.6
May 1	Frank Walshaw	Newtown	w.pts.6
May 11	Mick Cowan	London	w.pts.6
Jun 1	Joe Farley	London	w.rsc.2
Jun 1	Eddie Keith	London	w.rsc.2
Jun 1	Denny Ball	London	w.pts.3
	(Won Novices' Heavyweight Comp)		
Jul 19	Denny Ball	Cardiff	w.pts.6
Sep 14	Jim Moran	Sheffield	w.pts.6
Sep 28	Dennis Lockton	Hanley	w.pts.6
Oct 11	Morry Bush	Haverfordwest	w.pts.8
Nov 8	Frank Walker	Leicester	w.rsc.1
Dec 7	Cliff Purnell	Walsall	w.pts.8

1955

Feb 1	Hugh McDonald	Willenhall	w.rtd.6
Feb 15	Cliff Purnell	Birmingham	w.pts.8
Feb 28	Joe Crickmar	Leicester	w.pts.8
Mar 15	Peter Bates	Birmingham	w.pts.10
Apr 26	Simon Templar	London	w.rsc.8
May 9	Ansell Adams	Leicester	w.pts.10
Jul 18	Baby de Voogd	Cardiff	w.ko.1
Aug 29	Uber Bacillieri	Cardiff	w.pts.10
Sep 13	Antonia Crosia	London	w.rsc.8
Oct 10	Al Bernard	Cardiff	w.rtd.2
Nov 15	Henry Cooper	London	w.pts.10
	(Elim. British Heavyweight Title)		

1956

Jan 16	Marcel Limage	Cardiff	w.pts.10
Mar 19	Gunter Nurnberg	Carmarthen	w.pts.10
May 7	Dick Richardson	Cardiff	w.pts.10
Aug 27	Johnny Williams	Maindy	w.pts.15
	(British Heavyweight Title)		

1957

Feb 19	Nino Valdes	London	l.rsc.1
May 28	Peter Bates	Doncaster	w.pts.12
Sep 17	Henry Cooper	London	w.pts.15
	(British Heavyweight Title)		
Nov 25	Joe Bygraves	Leicester	w.pts.15
	(British Empire Heavyweight Title)		

1958

Feb 21	Ingemar Johansson	Gothenburg	l.rtd.13
	(European Heavyweight Title)		
Jun 3	Brian London	London	l.ko.8
	(British and Empire Heavyweight Titles)		
Nov 12	Max Brianto	Cardiff	w.pts.10

1959

Feb 24	Willie Pastrano	Wembley	w.pts.10
Jun 24	Dick Richardson	Coney Beach	w.pts.10
Aug 26	Bruno Scarabellin	Coney Beach	w.pts.10
Nov 17	Henry Cooper	London	l.rsc.12
	(British and Empire Heavyweight Titles)		

1960

Sep 22	Jose Gonzales	Cardiff	w.rsc.5

1961

Jan 24	Ulli Ritter	Leicester	w.pts.10
Mar 21	Henry Cooper	Wembley	l.rtd.5
	(British and Empire Heavyweight Titles)		
Oct 2	George Chuvalo	Toronto	w.dis.5

1962

Apr 2	Henry Cooper	Nottingham	l.rsc.9
	(British and Empire Heavyweight Titles)		
Nov 20	Mariano Echevarria	Leicester	w.pts.10
Dec 12	Alex Barrow	Blackpool	w.rsc.7

1963

Jul 29	Ray Cillien	Cardiff	w.rsc.4
Aug 10	Freddy Mack	Newtown	w.pts.10
Oct 13	Karl Mildenberger	Dortmund	l.pts.10

1964

Mar 3	Jack Bodell	Leicester	w.pts.10
Apr 21	Johnny Prescott	Birmingham	w.pts.10
Oct 27	Billy Walker	Wembley	l.pts.10

JOE ERSKINE
Heavy Weight Champion Gt. Britain

Manager: Benny Jacobs

CRAELY
CARDIFF

Joe Erskine

Joe Erskine weighs in for his contest against Dick Richardson.
pic: Royal Oak Collection

Willie Pastrano (left) v Joe Erskine

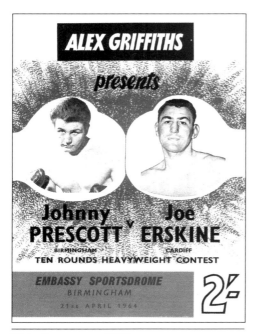

Fight Programme 1964

Fight Programme 1964

Chapter 6

Aryee Jackson was born in Ghana, where he began his professional career in 1955. Later that year he came to Wales and was looked after by Benny Jacobs and made his first appearance here against Ron Atkins, who was stopped in the second round of their contest at the Market Hall, Abergavenny.

He boxed just twenty-eight times in a thirteen year career but there are some interesting names on his record. In May 1957 he lost on points over ten rounds to Percy Lewis. A month previously, Lewis had been beaten on points over fifteen rounds by the Nigerian Hogan Bassey at Nottingham in a challenge for the Empire title, but before the end of the year Lewis took the Empire Featherweight title by stopping Charlie Hill in the tenth round, again at Nottingham.

On April 15th, 1959 Aryee beat John O`Brien on points in an eight rounder in Cardiff with O`Brien later going on to challenge Howard Winstone for the British title.

In June 1961 Jackson beat Phil Jones on points over eight rounds in Cardiff and on August 24th he was matched with Howard Winstone at Liverpool Stadium. Promoter Mickey Duff was delighted to secure the contest but thought that Eddie Thomas, Winstone`s manager would have rejected Jackson as an opponent as it was felt that Jackson`s swinging attacks might upset Winstone`s rhythm, but the contest was far from being a classic. Boxing News expressed the view that this was an unusual top-liner and Tim Riley wrote: "Although Jackson is not a famous name in boxing, he is a highly competent performer and this has resulted in most of the country`s leading featherweights being "unavailable" when his name is mentioned as a possible opponent."

Sid Bailey, in the South Wales Echo wrote: "Its tough on a boxer to win practically every round and then be booed from the ring.

That is what happened to Merthyr`s British Featherweight Champion Howard Winstone at Liverpool Stadium last night after he had clearly outpointed Aryee Jackson of Ghana over ten rounds.

The trouble was that the style of Jackson – if you can call it a style – did not blend with that of Winstone. So we had a spoiling, messy fight which at times had both men leaning on each other and mauling like all-in wrestlers.

Winstone himself said afterwards, "Jackson is like an octopus – he won`t let you box." That just about sums it up.

Jackson kept coming in, both arms working like windmills and at close quarters clutching Winstone at every opportunity.

Even so, the champion landed sufficient correct punches, especially in the first few rounds, to establish an unassailable points lead and there was no justification for the crowd's hostile demonstration at the end."

According to Boxing News the "contest fell far below the expected standard, although the British Champion opened in sparkling manner and always showed the superior ringcraft. But the vital snap was missing"

Steve Fagan, writing in the "Daily Sketch" observed: "The fight had a pattern by the fourth round, with the coloured boy forcing Winstone to the ropes, tossing punches at a terrific pace – but finding Winstone's defence impregnable."

Jackson jolted Winstone's head with two hooks at the start of the fifth round and he gave Howard little room to manoeuvre with his all-action style, but his successes were sporadic, with Howard sticking to his task and taking no chances as he coasted to victory.

Victory for Howard ensured that he was able to move onwards and upwards. Meanwhile, Aryee beat George Bowes on points over ten rounds and the return resulted in a draw over eight rounds. He later registered a win over Con Mount Bassie but after being stopped in a round by Jimmy Revie in 1967 and a points loss to Ken Cooper in February, 1968 Aryee Jackson retired, but nothing should detract from the fact that, at his peak, he was capable of extending the very best men in the featherweight division.

Aryee Jackson

Featherweight
Born: Ghana, 1934

1955

Apr 2	Sugar Gibiliru	Tarkwa, Ghan	w.ko.2
Jul 9	Sugar Gibiliru	Tarkwa, Ghana	l.ko.6
Nov 7	Ron Atkins	Abergavenny	w.rsc.2

1956

Feb 27	Teddy Barke	Cardiff	w.pts.6
Apr 9	Percy Lewis	Oxford	l.pts.8
Sep 24	Alf Drew	Oxford	w.pts.8
Oct 22	Ken Lawrence	Great Yarmouth	w.rsc.4
Nov 20	Jimmy Black	Streatham	w.pts.8

1957

Feb 20	Matt Fulton	Glasgow	w.pts.8
Apr 10	Matt Fulton	Paisley	w.pts.10
May 27	Percy Lewis	Cardiff	l.pts.10
Jul 15	Ernie Fossey	Abergavenny	w.pts.8
Aug 21	Denny Dawson	Cross Keys	w.rtd.4
Oct 7	Aime Devisch	Nottingham	w.pts.8

1958

Jan 14	Johnny Howard	Empress Hall, Earls Court	l.pts.8

1959

Apr 15	John O`Brien	Cardiff	w.pts.8
Jun 29	Max Murphy	Sydney	w.rsc.5
Jul 10	Steve Nitties	Melbourne	w.pts.12

1961

Apr 4	Tony Icke	Wolverhampton	w.pts.8
Jun 21	Phil Jones	Cardiff	w.pts.8
Aug 24	Howard Winstone	Liverpool	l.pts.10

1962

Jan 29	Louis Omberto	Cardiff	w.pts.8
Dec 4	George Bowes	Leeds	w.pts.10

1963

Aug 27	George Bowes	London	d.8

1964

Nov 25	Con Mount Bassie	Solihull	w.pts.8

1965

Inactive

1966

Mar 22	Billy Williams	Wolverhampton	d.pts.8

1967

Jun 27	Jimmy Revie	Shoreditch	l.rsc.1

1968

Feb 6	Ken Cooper	Wolverhampton	l.pts.8

Aryee Jackson

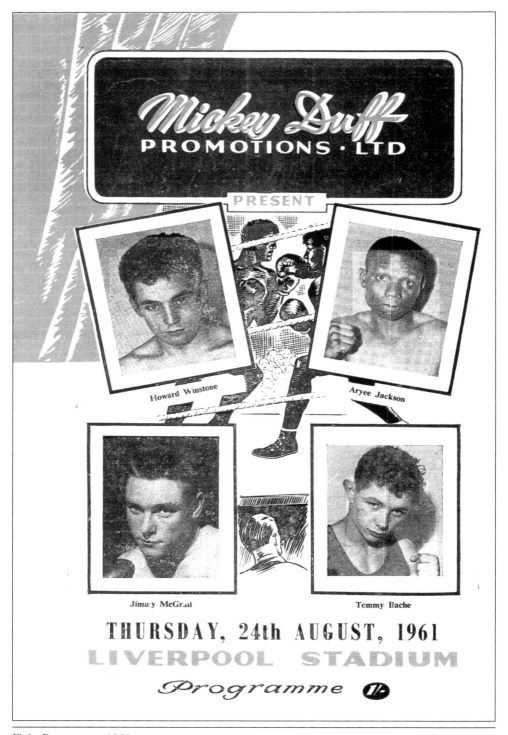

Fight Programme 1961

Chapter 7

Ronnie Rush was born in Grenada on December 4th, 1934, and only took up boxing at the age of 18. In barely a dozen contests he was amateur champion of Trinidad but decided to come to Wales in 1956 in the company of Eddie Bee and Egbert Jordan. All three joined Benny`s gym and Benny, showing his customary gift for spotting opportunities for publicity labelled them "The Calypso Kids", and the press quickly latched on to this. They even formed their own Steel Band in the gym and would turn out at fund-raising events such as the annual fete at the St. Lawrence Hospital in Chepstow.

Egbert Jordan was a heavyweight and boxed just three times, his final contest being a second round stoppage at the hands of Redvers Sangoe.

Eddie Bee, born in Trinidad on April 8th, 1934, boxed at welterweight and between 1956 and 1959 engaged in twentyfive contests meeting the likes of Johnny Griffin, Tex Woodward, Boswell St. Louis, Tony Smith and Mick Leahy.

Ronnie boxed as a lightweight and fought thirtyfive times between 1956 and 1962. His record shows just fifteen wins but he enjoyed regular work and even had three contests in Australia during 1959. He dropped into the role of "journeyman fighter" but he faced many of the leading names in the lightweight division on the domestic front including Al Sharpe and Dave Stone who was disqualified in the fourth round of their contest in London.

His final contest came in February, 1962, when he was stopped by Tanos Lambrianidies, also from the Jacobs` stable, in the sixth round at Maesteg.

It is fair to say that Ronnie`s finest achievements in boxing have come as a trainer. Since finding his way back into the sport he has trained countless amateur boxers in the tough Ely district of Cardiff but he also trained Steve Robinson and Barry Jones, both of whom won WBO titles at Featherweight and Superfeatherweight respectively.

Steve worked as a £60 per week storeman in Cardiff before he was given the opportunity, with just 48 hours notice, to challenge for the world title. The word was that Steve had just eaten a meal of pie and chips when the phone rang with the offer of the contest, but Steve was always superbly fit, something he retains to this day, and history shows that he took the opportunity with both hands in beating John Davison on points in their battle up in the North East.

Steve Robinson went on to defend his title successfully seven times, defeating former champions Paul Hodkinson, Colin McMillan and Duke McKenzie before finally losing his title to Naseem Hamed. Sadly, the relationship between Ronnie and Steve deteriorated, but Ronnie was to groom another world champion in Cardiff's Barry Jones.

Barry won his title against Wilson Palacios on points over twelve rounds at Millwall in December, 1997, but unfortunately, problems with his annual brain scan and a lengthy dispute with the boxing authorities kept him out of the ring for some time. He returned to the ring in June 1999 with a points win over Chris Williams at the Cardiff International Arena, a contest which I had the pleasure of refereeing, and on January 15th, 2000, he was given the opportunity of challenging for his old title when he was matched with the awesome Brazilian Acelino "Popo" Freitas at Doncaster, but sadly for Barry, he was stopped in the eighth round.

Nothing can detract from Ronnie's achievements on this front and he can still be seen working the corner for the young boxers from his gym.

In April, 1998, Ronnie was honoured for his work by the Variety Club of Great Britain when they staged a tribute dinner at the Marriott Hotel in Cardiff, and having refereed several of his boxers over the years I was delighted to be invited along. His contribution to boxing has been immense, but so too has been his contribution to the local community.

Ronnie Rush

Lightweight
Cardiff
Born: Trinidad, December 4th, 1934

1956

Jun 18	Dave Savva	Birmingham	w.rsc.5
Jul 7	Johnny McMullen	Aberystwyth	w.pts.6
Aug 23	Bob Roberts	Liverpool Stad.	w.pts.4
Oct 1	Ansong Mensah	Walsall	w.rsc.2
Oct 22	Ray Akwei	Derby	w.pts.8
Nov 5	Andy Baird	Walsall	w.pts.8
Nov 12	Bryn Phillips	Cardiff	l.dis.1

1957

Mar 5	Stan Skinkiss	Birmingham	l.pts.8
May 6	Al Sharpe	Newcastle	l.rsc.6
Jun 24	Derek Clarke	Carlisle	w.ko.2
Jul 15	Johnny McMullen	Abergavenny	w.pts.6
Sep 2	Tommy Mason	Maesteg	w.ko.1
Oct 28	Arty McGill	Neath	w.rsc.6
Nov 4	Brian Jones	Walsall	l.pts.6
Dec 12	Tommy McGuiness	Cheltenham	l.pts.8

1958

Jan 27	Harry Edwards	Banbury	w.pts.8
Mar 3	Ebe Mensah	Walsall	l.rsc.5
Apr 22	Eddie Hughes	Manor Place Baths	w.ko.3
Sep 9	Ebe Mensah	Birmingham	d.pts.8
Sep 30	Johnny Kidd	Harringay	l.pts.8
Nov 12	Ray Ashie	Cardiff	d.pts.8

1959

Feb 4	Ray Ashie	Cardiff	l.rtd.4
Mar 9	Brian Husband	Halifax	l.rsc.3
Mar 19	Tony Smith	Liverpool	l.pts.8
Apr 3	Ray Corbett	Banbury	w.rsc.2
Apr 15	Johnny Melfah	Cardiff	d.8
Jun 26	Alf O'Sullivan	Melbourne	d.12
Jul 3	Alf O'Sullivan	Melbourne	l.rsc.10
Jul 20	Brian Sheehan	Sydney	l.rsc.4
Nov 23	Brian Jones	Banbury	l.pts.8

1960

Mar 1	Dave Stone	London	w.dis.4
Mar 14	Johnny Van Rensburg	London	l.pts.8
Jun 13	Ron Hinson	London	l.rtd.5

1962

Feb 12	Tanos Lambrianides	Maesteg	l.rsc.6

Ronnie Rush

Chapter 8

Redvers Sangoe was born in Tiger Bay and as a young boy he went to St. Mary's School later transferring to South Church Street School. Some of his school friends would later become his stable-mates, namely Joe Erskine, whose father taught Redvers to box, Phil Edwards and Teddy Best but his friends also included Billy Boston and Johnny Freeman, men who would go on to become stars in Rugby League.

Redvers started boxing at the age of twelve and won a Welsh schoolboys' title. Later, he went on to become British Army Lightheavyweight Champion but the professional career of Redvers Sangoe did not get off to the best of starts. His first contest took place on July 16th, 1956 at Maindy Stadium, Cardiff and he was knocked out in the first round by Danny Wall. His second contest was staged at the Market Hall in Abergavenny in October and his opponent was Cliff Purnell, a former opponent of Henry Cooper, who beat Redvers on points over six rounds but after this inauspicious start, 1957 turned out to be a much better year.

Having started his professional career with Eddie Dumazel he switched to Benny's gym and his fortunes changed almost immediately. He boxed eleven times, losing just once, and by November he was in contention for the Lightheavyweight Championship of Wales. In January, he stopped Egbert Jordan in two rounds in Cardiff and in March he stopped Peter Woodward in the first round at Birmingham. Barely two weeks later, he knocked out Ken Gardner in the fourth round in Cardiff and his career began to gain momentum. Points victories followed over Colin Strauch and Dennis Lockton, a former opponent of Joe Erskine, but on June 4th he lost on points to Ron Redrup at Harringay. He returned to winning ways in July beating Cliff Purnell again at Abergavenny and on August 21st, he beat Johnny Williamson on points over eight rounds at Cross Keys. Following his fifth round disqualification win over Abe Stanley at Preston he was matched with Don Sainsbury in Cardiff in an eliminator for the Welsh Lightheavyweight title. He forced Sainsbury to retire in the eighth round and he ended the year by forcing Jack London Jr into retirement in the sixth round of their contest at Leeds.

He returned to Leeds for his first contest of 1958 and knocked out Eddie Ted Williams in the fourth round. Next up was Basil Kew who was beaten on points over eight rounds at Carmarthen and less than three weeks later he was in action again in Hull, this time losing on points to Jack London.

On March 31st, he took his third contest of the month and lost on points over eight rounds to Neville Rowe in Leeds but on April 23rd, he challenged Noel Trigg for the Lightheavyweight Championship of Wales in Cardiff and took the title with a win on points over twelve rounds.

At the weigh-in at the Royal Hotel, Sangoe scaled12st. 7lbs while Trigg, from Newport came in at 12st. 4.1/2lbs. When the first bell rang, Sophia Gardens Pavilion was packed to capacity and the contest was relayed to about 8,000 patients listening on the East Wales Hospital Broadcast System.

His win over the champion, Trigg, was considered to be something of an upset as he outclassed his opponent in their battle over twelve mauling, brawling rounds.

Trigg was the cleaner puncher and began the fight confidently, but he began to wilt dramatically around the half-way mark allowing the plodding Sangoe to take the final rounds and the title.

Though a little slow, Sangoe was effective and he employed a combination of left jab and right counter which staggered Trigg, notably in the eighth round, and at the final bell Sangoe was a worthy winner.

In May he travelled to Glasgow where he lost to Dave Mooney on points over eight rounds and on July 22nd he faced Randolph Turpin at Oswestry. The glory days of Turpin were long gone and it was seven years on from that glorious night at Earls Court when he beat the legendary Sugar Ray Robinson to cap one of the finest nights in British boxing history. He was now nearing the end of his career but he had recently defeated Eddie Wright in seven rounds suggesting that he was still a force to be reckoned with on the home front and reinforcing this, Turpin stopped Redvers in the fourth round. For Randolph Turpin, there was to be just one more contest when sadly, he was knocked out in two rounds by Yolande Pompey.

The contest between Sangoe and Turpin took place at Oswestry football ground and the match was made at 12st 12lbs.

The promoters Alex Griffiths and Joe Jacobs were interested in staging the bout between Turpin and Pompey and to protect their interests took out an option for a Sangoe v Pompey contest at Leicester should Sangoe beat Turpin.

Sangoe had every reason for disposing of Turpin in quick time. Indeed, there was a clause in his contract that would pay him an extra £200 pounds should he topple the British Champion, but on the down side, Redvers was set to lose £100 if he were to be stopped inside the distance.

The Western Mail report of the contest ran as follows: "Randolph Turpin, the British Lightheavyweight Champion made short work of Redvers Sangoe, the Welsh Champion from Tiger Bay, Cardiff, at Oswestry last night.

Sangoe took a count of eight in the third round and of seven and nine in the fourth before the referee intervened.

It was Turpin`s vicious right hooks to the body which did the damage, but the end came when Turpin landed a hard left on Sangoe`s left eye which brought blood spurting from it, and then quickly followed it with another tremendous left to the body.

Sangoe went down, blinded by blood; he tried to continue, but was in no fit state.

Sangoe opened the fight with a flurry of blows, but Turpin almost casually warded him off.

There was little power in Sangoe`s punches, but once, he caught Turpin in a corner. However, Turpin, with classic ease, turned the tables, and at the bell it was Sangoe who was on the receiving end in the corner.

At the start of the second round, blood started to seep from Turpin`s mouth, but his injury was slight.

It was at this stage that Turpin began to bring his right into action, and Sangoe could find no defence to Turpin`s body punching, consisting of perfectly placed, vicious right hooks with an occasional left for good measure.

The third round saw the beginning of the end. Turpin, going forward menacingly, suddenly started to pound away relentlessly at Sangoe`s heart.

Turpin flung five wicked right hooks in quick succession, and Sangoe dropped like a stone. At the count of eight he was up, and Turpin, rather surprisingly seemed to ease.

At the start of the fourth round Turpin really got to work and chopped Sangoe down for a count of seven before splitting Sangoe`s right eyelid and then dropping him with one of his frequent left hooks".

This was a serious beating for Redvers while Turpin went on to meet Pompey in September and was crushed in two rounds finally bringing to an end the career of the "Leamington Licker".

After a few months of inactivity Redvers Sangoe was back in the ring on January 12th, 1959 when he faced Chic Calderwood at the Empress Hall, Earls Court. Topping the bill was Henry Cooper, who took the British and Empire Heavyweight titles from Brian London with a points win over fifteen rounds. Calderwood was rapidly emerging as one of the best lightheavyweights in the country and had recently stopped Dave Mooney to take the Scottish title and in his previous contest had forced Neville Rowe to retire in six rounds. Career-wise, the momentum was with Chic and he stopped Sangoe in the fifth round.

Redvers took a painful beating from the Caigneuk fighter before being rescued by the referee. Sangoe took everything the undefeated Scot threw at him until he sustained a nasty gash under the chin which clearly handicapped him from the second round onwards.

Sangoe was put down for a count of nine in the fourth round while in the fifth round he went to the canvas four times for lengthy counts before the referee mercifully intervened.

Following a points win over Ted Williams, Redvers was matched with the experienced Ron Barton, who had won the British Lightheavyweight title in 1956 by beating Albert Finch. The contest was staged at Streatham Ice Rink with Barton taking the decision and he followed this with a win over Garnett Denny in the Eisteddfod marquee at Colwyn Bay. There was plenty of action as both men slugged it out in a small ring in front of a crowd of 2,500 fans. Denny was floored for a count of nine in the second round but fought back to take the fifth and the sixth. Later, Sangoe seemed upset by a warning to keep his punches up but got back on top again to secure the decision.

Redvers went on to defend his Welsh title against Don Sainsbury at Aberdare with Sainsbury being forced to retire in the ninth round and their rematch in Carmarthen six months later ended with an identical result.

The contest against Sainsbury at Aberdare was promoted by Theo Davies of Merthyr and Redvers weighed in at 12st. 6lbs while Sainsbury, from Penarth, scaled 12st. 7lbs. The bill also featured the match between Terry Rees and Gordon Blakey for the Welsh Featherweight title and Howard Winstone faced Billy Calvert of Sheffield.

Redvers, showing a recent improvement outclassed the plucky Sainsbury who had battled doggedly for nine rounds.

Sainsbury, managed by Nat Seller, had little left as the eighth round ended but came out for the ninth round determined to battle on in spite of a badly swollen left eye.

The speed of Sangoe was impressive and his left hand was extremely effective, so much so, that Sainsbury could only move in close in an attempt to negate its effect.

In the sixth round Sainsbury made a huge effort to turn the tide in his favour and caught Sangoe with some piercing lefts and vicious right crosses almost forcing the champion through the ropes in the process, but Redvers weathered the storm and as the contest ran its course, so he increased his points lead. There is no doubt he was well ahead when referee Ike Powell stepped between them in the ninth round.

In April he lost on points to Gerry McNally at Oxford and on July 27th, 1960 he was stopped in three rounds by Jack Whittaker at Coney Beach Arena, Porthcawl in what turned out to be his final contest.

Topping the bill was Dick Richardson against Mike DeJohn. The American had based himself at the Royal Hotel in Cardiff and did his training at Benny`s gym. Redvers sparred with the visitor and according to Lennie Williams and Harry Carroll, the American had no idea how to cope with Sangoe. Redvers had an impressive physique and had strong powerful legs. He had an excellent jab and showed good movement in the ring but in reality, he was a great gym-fighter. The younger boxers at the gym learned a great deal from him as he handled Joe Erskine and Phil Edwards with ease. Brian Curvis sparred at the gym from time to time and he too was handled comfortably by Redvers. As with many boxers he suffered badly with nerves on fight night, and in some ways this is puzzling because he was one of the great characters of the gym and was always laughing and smiling but nerves obviously prevented him from reaching his full potential.

He went on to become a partner in a general store in Butetown. He was married with one child and the family home had been in Dudley Street, in the Dock area.

The story of Redvers Sangoe ended in tragedy at about 7.pm on August 14th, 1964. Lennie Williams tells of Redvers leaving the gym in his usual happy-go-lucky style to return to his home in Tiger Bay. Later, Teddy Best arrived at the gym with the news that Redvers had been stabbed. As Benny Jacobs was taking Lennie back to his hotel in Newport Road they stopped off at Cardiff Royal Infirmary to check on his condition, only to be met with the news that Redvers had just been pronounced dead.

This came as a huge shock to everyone who knew him and Harry Carroll, who was a good friend of his, insists that even though he was a tough man inside the ropes, he was not a violent man outside the ring.

On Saturday, August 15th, a Jamaican labourer was charged with his murder and remanded in custody at Cardiff Magistrates Court, which was packed for the hearing. Redvers died from stab-wounds to the chest, but the South Wales Echo reported that he was taken initially to Bute Street police station, from where he was transferred to hospital where he was pronounced dead on arrival.

During a court hearing about a month later it became clear that there had been trouble between the two men in the past. There was a quarrel over a woman who at one time was a friend of Sangoe, but who, at the time in question was living with the accused. On the night of the attack eye-witnesses claimed that Sangoe "was not armed in any way but was fighting as though he was boxing". Later, during a search of the home of the accused, a bloodstained pen-knife was found. When questioned, he stated that he had been afraid to admit to using the knife when he heard that Sangoe was dead.

The Jamaican was sent for trial at the Glamorgan Assizes but his legal representative, Sir Charles Hallinan submitted that his client should not be sent for trial on a charge of murder since in his view the evidence pointed to Sangoe as the aggressor and assailant.

Boxing often throws up the "Rags to Riches" story but there is also a darker side and the lightheavyweight division in Britain has seen its share of tragedy. Following the death of Redvers Sangoe, Freddie Mills, the former Lightheavyweight Champion of the World was to die in suspicious circumstances, Randolph Turpin, former Middleweight Champion of the World and winner of a Lonsdale Belt at lightheavyweight is believed to have committed suicide following a final demand from the Inland Revenue and Chic Calderwood died in a car crash. Fighters are special people who give so much of themselves in the ring and deserve better than a violent end.

Redvers Sangoe

Lightheavyweight
Cardiff
Born: July 6th, 1936

1956

Jul 16	Danny Wall	Maindy	l.ko.1
Oct 29	Cliff Purnell	Abergavenny	l.pts.6

1957

Jan 16	Egbert Jordan	Cardiff	w.rsc.2
Mar 5	Peter Woodward	Birmingham	w.rsc.1
Mar 18	Ken Gardner	Cardiff	w.ko.4
Apr 16	Colin Strauch	Rotherham	w.pts.6
May 27	Dennis Lockton	Cardiff	w.pts.6
Jun 4	Ron Redrup	London	l.pts.6
Jul 15	Cliff Purnell	Abergavenny	w.pts.6
Aug 21	Johnny Williamson	Cross Keys	w.pts.8
Oct 14	Abe Stanley	Preston	w.dis.5
Nov 11	Don Sainsbury	Cardiff	w.rtd.8
	(Elim. Welsh Lightheavyweight Title)		
Dec 9	Jack London	Leeds	w.rtd.6

1958

Feb 10	Eddie Ted Williams	Leeds	w.ko.4
Mar 3	Basil Kew	Carmarthen	w.pts.8
Mar 20	Jack London	Hull	l.pts.8
Mar 31	Neville Rowe	Leeds	l.pts.8
Apr 23	Noel Trigg	Cardiff	w.pts.12
	(Welsh Lightheavyweight Title)		
May 21	Dave Mooney	Glasgow	l.pts.8
Jul 22	Randolph Turpin	Oswestry	l.rsc.4

1959

Jan 12	Chic Calderwood	London	l.rsc.5
Mar 9	Ted Williams	Halifax	w.pts.8
Mar 24	Ron Barton	London	l.pts.8
Aug 22	Garnett Denny	Colwyn Bay	w.pts.8
Sep 1	Don Sainsbury	Aberdare	w.rtd.9
	(Welsh Lightheavyweight Title)		

1960

Mar 21	Don Sainsbury	Carmarthen	w.rtd.9
	(Welsh Lightheavyweight Title)		
Apr 4	Gerry McNally	Oxford	l.pts.8
Jul 27	Jack Whittaker	Coney Beach	l.rsc.3

Redvers Sangoe

Redvers Sangoe (left) with Gordon Blakey, Joe Erskine & Ernie Hurford.
Pic: Courtesy of Gordon Blakey

Chapter 9

Ron "Ponty" Davies enjoyed an extremely successful amateur career representing the Army and Wales and in 1955 he captured the Welsh ABA Flyweight title.

On April 26th, 1957 he won the ABA Flyweight Championship when he beat D. Lloyd (New Buxton) on points in the final while Malcolm Collins of Cardiff became champion at featherweight and Dave Thomas took the heavyweight crown in a remarkable year for Welsh boxers.

Ron decided to turn professional with Benny Jacobs and he made his debut at the Market Hall, Abergavenny on July 15th, 1957. His opponent was Barry Adgie, who was stopped in the third round. Adgie was a capable fighter who would go on to meet Don James, Errol Flynn and Don Braithwaite in a career that stretched to fifty-one contests.

"Ponty" displayed an exceptional work-rate and it was clear from the outset that he was anxious to impress. Adgie had little to offer in the face of all-out aggression and was bewildered by the punches that were coming towards him from all angles.

Adgie was virtually wrestled over in the first round and in the second, he was floored for a count of nine. When he rose the torrent of punches continued with Adgie unable to cope with the Welshman`s speed of hand and foot and there was a sense of relief when the stoppage came in the third round.

He was back in action at Coney Beach Arena, Porthcawl just two weeks later and once again confirmed himself as a rough, tough prospect when he hammered the game Frank Spencer to defeat in the fifth round. "Ponty" waded in from the first bell swinging lefts and rights furiously and even ended up on the floor himself after throwing a big right hand. He was so anxious to crush his opponent he was warned in the second round for hitting on the back of the head.

Spencer was baffled by his opponent`s unorthodox style as he frequently changed from southpaw and back while hammering away.

Spencer went down for a count of eight in the second round and was punished severely in rounds three and four as Davies rained in punches from all angles. Spencer had no idea how to handle this level of aggression. By now, his left eye was badly cut and after taking another count in the fifth round, the referee had seen enough.

On September 3rd, 1958 Davies registered his best win to date when he stopped Len "Luggie" Reece in the seventh round at Coney Beach Arena though Reece was well ahead on points when the end came and had fought from the first round with blood flowing from a cut over his left eye.

Reece displayed a classical boxing style and kept drawing Davies on to punches and clipping him hard, and time and again, his left hand found its way through the defence of Davies, while "Ponty" used his strength to keep boring forward.

The Llanbradach miner was halted occasionally by Reece, but maintained his forward momentum and would not be denied.

Davies showed no respect for the reputation of Reece and in the heat of battle he was warned for using the heel of the glove and later for misuse of the head. He stuck doggedly to his task and by working away at the injury, he achieved his goal.

On February 4th, 1959 Phil Edwards faced Martin Hansen at Sophia Gardens with Ponty due to appear on the undercard against the Indian Pancho Bhatachaji, but much of the pre-fight publicity centred on the withdrawal of Davies from the promotion. He was contracted to box at 8st. 3lbs and in the week before the contest he was down to 8st. 5.3/4lbs. He trained on the Thursday evening but did not turn up for his roadwork on Friday and when he failed to show up for his gym session Benny went to his lodgings in Ninian Park Road only to be told by the landlady that Ponty had gone out at lunchtime and had not returned. On Saturday, promoter Stan Cottle, matchmaker Harry Gorman and Benny set out by car to track down Ponty. They spoke to his mother who said he had gone to Newport with friends, but in a scene resembling something out of the "Keystone Cops", Stan, Harry and Benny tracked him down to a pub in Caerphilly. Ponty had a pint glass in front of him and had clearly been drinking cider, though he maintained it was fruit juice and with his own inimitable humour Benny confirmed that the apple was indeed a fruit!

Stan Cottle swore that he would never allow Ponty to appear on one of his shows again, though when Ponty was check-weighed on the Sunday he was just over 9st.5lb and he contacted Mr E. J. Waltham, the secretary of the British Boxing Board of Control to say that he was prepared to appear on the show but boxing at featherweight as a gesture of good faith to the promoter, but clearly, Ponty knew he could not get down to the poundage originally agreed for this contest. The end result was a lengthy period of inactivity.

"Ponty" returned to the ring on June 14th, 1960 with a hastily arranged contest against Eddie Barraclough at Penydarren Park, Merthyr Tydfil. The Rotherham fighter was then rated fifth in the Bantamweight division. Even though Davies was in good physical condition he had only completed four rounds of sparring in preparation for this fight but showed that he had lost none of his fighting spirit. The crowd was treated to eight blistering rounds and even though he missed at times and looked to be out of breath at the halfway mark, he boxed well and took a clear points win from referee Joe Morgan.

Barraclough stormed forward throwing punches and he was warned by the referee when "Ponty" was hurt badly at the end of the fifth round but Davies then stormed forward, forcing his opponent to back-pedal during the later stages of the fight.

Two months later, "Ponty" caused one of the boxing sensations of the year by outpointing British Flyweight Champion Frankie Jones at Aberdare.

The Llanbradach man showed dogged determination throughout and finally prevailed over a boxing artist. He kept moving forward throughout and his reward was victory over the champion in only his sixth professional fight and this caused speculation as to whether he might face Jones again with the title at stake, or whether he might face Risto Luukkonen of Finland, the European Champion.

The first round was fairly evenly contested but Jones took rounds two and three with some good left-hand work. Davies came back to take rounds four and five and showed he was capable of fighting back when hurt.

Fortunes swayed again when Jones came back to take the sixth and seventh rounds. He was able to ride "Ponty`s" punches and coped well against the strength of the Welshman inside, but gradually the strength of Davies became a crucial factor and began to take its toll with Jones beginning to show signs of concern.

Ponty was now throwing punches from all angles and the Scot realised that he would have to stand toe to toe to have any chance of success.

His work was accurate but at the final bell, referee Bill Jones raised the arm of Davies after an extremely close contest. Joe Gans, the champion`s manager thought they had done enough to win, but this result was a huge boost for Ponty.

Shortly before his next fight against Pancho Bhatachaji at Sophia Gardens Pavilion, there was talk of "Ponty" facing former amateur opponent Derek Lloyd over ten rounds at 8st 2lb for promoter Harry Levene at Wembley and Benny had also been in conversation with Johnny de John, manager of heavyweight Mike and also manager of Carmen Basilio with a view to taking Phil Edwards and "Ponty" to the States.

Bhatachaji, who had knocked out British Champion Frankie Jones and had lost a disputed decision in Finland to European Champion Risto Luukkonen, proved to be the toughest fight to date for Davies.

He boxed coolly and refused to be intimidated by "Ponty`s" aggressive style and was happy to punch it out.

Davies paced himself admirably and looked to be well on top when the end came. Bhatachaji was cut between the eyes and the power of Davies` punches opened further cuts over both eyes.

In the fateful seventh round, the Indian dropped his guard and took more heavy punishment from the Welshman thus prompting the visitor`s corner to signal their retirement.

A return would have been a mouth-watering attraction, but sadly, it did not happen. Neither did the proposed fight at Wembley, nor the trip to the States, with "Ponty" deciding he was through with boxing.

Ron "Ponty" Davies

Flyweight
Llanbradach
Born: October 19th, 1937
Welsh ABA Flyweight Champion, 1955
ABA Flyweight Champion, 1957

1957

| Jul 15 | Barry Adgie | Abergavenny | w.rsc.3 |
| Jul 31 | Frankie Spencer | Porthcawl | w.rsc.5 |

1958

May 17	Jim Brennan	Belfast	w.rsc.2
Jul 9	Davey Moore	Coney Beach	w.rsc.3
Sep 3	Len Reece	Coney Beach	w.rsc.7

1960

Jun 14	Eddie Barraclough	Merthyr	w.pts.8
Aug 15	Frankie Jones	Aberdare	w.pts.10
Sep 22	Pancho Bhatachaji	Cardiff	w.rtd.7

PONTY DAVIES (Llanbradach)
Fly Weight

Manager:
BENNY JACOBS

CRAELY, CARDIFF

Ponty Davies

Chapter 10

One of the highlights of Gordon Blakey`s amateur career was winning the Welsh ABA Bantamweight title in 1955.

He turned professional with Benny Jacobs in 1957 and made his professional debut at Cross Keys on August 21st, stopping Sammy Cosgrove in the fifth round. The contest featured on the undercard of a double Welsh title bill when Phil Edwards challenged Freddie Cross and Teddy Best challenged Bryn Phillips. Many thought Blakey`s performance was the most impressive of the night and Cosgrove was reeling and bleeding badly when referee Jim Brimmell intervened. He was in action again in Cardiff less than three weeks later when he beat Joe Sharp on points over four rounds and he saw out the year with points victories over Billy Allport and Terry Coles at Cheltenham and Gloucester respectively.

During 1958 he engaged in ten contests winning all but two. February was a busy month which began with a points win over Colin Salcombe at Walsall. Two weeks later he beat Roy Taylor on points over eight rounds at Kettering and a week later, he beat Terry Rees on points over six rounds at Harringay in the first of four meetings.

Following wins over Lol Reaney in Birmingham and Terry Rees in Cardiff he tasted defeat for the first time against Trevor Martin in Belfast when he was knocked out in the first round. He returned to action with a points win over Ken Hignett at Oswestry and then lost on points over six rounds to Terry Rees at Maindy Stadium.

On November 27th, he beat Billy Graydon on points over six rounds in London and he ended the year by stopping Billy Allport at the National Sporting Club in three rounds.

Gordon returned to action in May, 1959, when he beat Alex Bryant on points over eight rounds in Cardiff. He followed this up with a points win over Jerry Parker before being matched with Terry Rees on September 1st for the Welsh Featherweight Title at the Ynys Sports Stadium, Aberdare. This was their fourth and final meeting and unfortunately for Gordon, he landed a low blow and was promptly disqualified in the sixth round leaving Terry and Gordon with two wins apiece.

There was a shock at the weigh-in when Rees came in six ounces over the featherweight limit while Gordon weighed in at 8st. 13.1/2 lbs. Terry returned to the scales an hour later and was then two ounces under the limit but he looked drawn as the first bell rang while Blakey looked the stronger of the two and he emphasised this in the opening round by taking the fight to Rees in typical two-handed style.

Terry Rees, originally from Blaencwm, Blaenrhondda, but based in Catford, relied on his piercing left jab and used the ring fluently, making Gordon miss from time to time.

Blakey was warned by referee Bernard Murphy as early as the first round for an alleged low-blow, but he continued to score with accurate left hooks to the midriff.

By the fifth round there was very little in it but Blakey stormed forward and dropped Rees for a count of five with a terrific body shot. Some of the crowd of around 1,500 felt that the blow was "south of the border", but Gordon, sensing he was getting on top became over-eager and slipped to the canvas.

The sixth round was a heated affair, and having received a warning from the referee for a low blow, Blakey waded into his man and threw another low blow which resulted in instant disqualification thus handing the title to Terry Rees. This was an unsatisfactory conclusion to a contest which had promised so much, with both boxers being so evenly matched.

In the past, winners of the Welsh title had nothing to show for their achievements and the Welsh Ex-Boxers` Association has attempted to rectify this in recent years. At their annual get-together in September 2006, Terry was presented with a championship belt to commemorate his achievement and his delight was clear for all to see on what was an extremely emotional day for him and his family.

On October 20th, Gordon forced Ollie Wyllie into fourth round retirement at Wembley on a bill which featured British Featherweight Champion Bobby Neill. Bobby faced the awesome American Davey Moore and was stopped in the first round.

During 1960 Gordon engaged in nine contests, winning five and losing four. On January 14th he beat Tommy Tiger on points over eight rounds in Cardiff and repeated his victory in March at Derby.

On March 31st, he was matched with Howard Winstone at Sophia Gardens, Cardiff, and the report of the contest in Boxing News ran as follows: "Generally agreed by a capacity Sophia Gardens Pavilion to be the best "feathers dust-up for years", the meeting of unbeaten Merthyr Tydfil featherweight prospect Howard Winstone and Cardiff rival Gordon Blakey saw the feathers flying with a vengeance before Blakey, right eye closed and bleeding, was forced to retire at the end of round eight.

Winstone (8st 13 and 13 lbs) was bustled out of his normal smooth-moving style by the two-fisted onslaughts of Blakey (9. 0.3/4 lbs), who caused a buzz of excited speculation by forcing Winstone on to the defensive from the first bell.

In the second round Blakey clobbered Winstone with a peach of a right to the jaw and followed it up with a barrage of lefts and rights to the head and body. Winstone showed plenty of ringcraft in riding this storm, but there was little doubt that Blakey had shaded the round.

The third round was another grand slam, with Blakey tossing over right handers that Winstone could not always parry; and, although the Merthyr man tried hard to get his favourite left jab working, Blakey got through with a right to the jaw and started an outsize "cauliflower" into bloom on Winstone`s left ear.

In the fourth round Blakey started offering his chin (an old and much criticised habit), and Winstone accepted the invitation and peppered left jabs to redden and bruise Blakey`s face.

Blakey had missed his chance of producing an upset victory in those sensational opening rounds, and Winstone, now in control, proceeded to hand out a boxing lesson.

In round seven it seemed to be all over bar the shouting as Blakey took repeated short rights and left hooks to the jaw and tottered visibly, as he backpedalled. Then, suddenly, he unshipped a tremendous right flush to Winstone`s jaw which jarred the Merthyr man into fighting back grimly to regain the initiative.

Round eight proved to be the last, and Winstone seemed to sense it. He stood up to a preliminary Blakey attack and then floored Gordon with a vicious left-right combination for "six".

Blakey looked to be in dire trouble, and Winstone piled on the pressure to flatten Blakey again for "six", the bell intervening when Blakey seemed woozy.

In the interval between rounds, referee Ike Powell went over to Blakey`s corner, where manager Benny Jacobs signalled that Blakey`s eye was too badly damaged for him to continue. There is some talk of a return at Coney Beach Arena, Porthcawl in June."

The return never materialised and Howard was left with a permanent reminder of their battle each time he looked in the mirror, but Gordon was back in action in May beating Eric Brett on points over eight rounds at Swansea. This contest took place at the Vetch Field and featured on the undercard of Brian Curvis beating Australian George Barnes for the Empire Welterweight title. Howard Winstone also featured on the bill and stopped George Carroll in four rounds.

In his next contest, Gordon beat Eric Baronet on points over eight rounds at Merthyr but in September, he was stopped in the sixth round of his contest against Hugh O`Neill at the National Sporting Club in London. Gordon was almost certainly heading for a win over the Irishman when he emerged from a clinch in the sixth round with blood streaming from a cut over his left eye and the referee had to stop the contest. Another defeat came in November at the hands of George Judge, but a fortnight later he stopped Rudy Edwards in the fifth round at Carmarthen. He ended the year with an appearance at Wembley on the undercard of the contest between Henry Cooper and Alex Miteff but sadly, he was stopped in the seventh round by Al McCarthy.

The year 1961 proved to be the last of his career. In March he beat Junior Cassidy on a disqualification at Maesteg and in June he stopped Paddy Kelly in the sixth round of their contest in Cardiff. Gordon was the more skilful and the stronger of the two, flooring Kelly for three counts during round six before the referee intervened, but his final contest came at Wembley on July 11th when Terry Downes won the Middleweight Championship of the World against American Paul Pender. Gordon`s opponent on the night was Danny O`Brien, and unfortunately, the Cardiff man was stopped in the sixth round.

Gordon has always been a popular member of the Welsh Ex-Boxers' Association and at the annual get-together of the Association he needs little encouragement to burst into song. His rendition of "I Had a Little Nut-Tree" is not to be missed and it was a pleasure to see him meet up with old sparring partner David Darkie Hughes at a function in Cardiff in 2006 to celebrate the retirement of trainer Charlie Pearson, the man who took Nicky Piper and Enzo Maccarinelli through to become champions. He also meets up with former stablemate Ron "Ponty" Davies every week at the Hayes Snack Bar in Cardiff no doubt reliving past battles and putting the world to right!

Gordon Blakey (left), Promoter Stan Cottle & Howard Winstone.
pic: Courtesy of Western Mail & Echo

Gordon Blakey

Featherweight
Cardiff
Born: August 21, 1937
Welsh ABA Bantamweight Champion, 1955

1957

Aug 21	Sammy Cosgrove	Cross Keys	w.rsc.5
Sep 9	Joe Sharp	Cardiff	w.pts.4
Dec 2	Billy Allport	Cheltenham	w.pts.6
Dec 9	Terry Coles	Gloucester	w.pts.6

1958

Feb 3	Colin Salcombe	Walsall	w.pts.6
Feb 17	Roy Taylor	Kettering	w.pts.8
Feb 25	Terry Rees	Harringay	w.pts.6
Apr 3	Lol Reaney	Birmingham	w.pts.6
Apr 23	Terry Rees	Cardiff	w.pts.6
May 17	Trevor Martin	Belfast	l.ko.1
Jul 22	Ken Hignett	Oswestry	w.pts.6
Nov 12	Terry Rees	Cardiff	l.pts.6
Nov 27	Billy Graydon	London	w.pts.6
Dec 29	Billy Allport	NSC	w.rsc.3

1959

May 27	Alex Bryant	Cardiff	w.pts.8
Jul 14	Jerry Parker	Aberdare	w.pts.8
Sep 1	Terry Rees	Aberdare	l.dis.6
	(Welsh Featherweight Title)		
Oct 20	Ollie Wyllie	Wembley	w.rtd.4

1960

Jan 14	Tommy Tiger	Cardiff	w.pts.8
Mar 21	Tommy Tiger	Derby	w.pts.8
Mar 31	Howard Winstone	Cardiff	l.rtd.8
May 9	Eric Brett	Swansea	w.pts.8
Jun 14	Eric Baronet	Merthyr	w.pts.8
Sep 12	Hugh O`Neill	London	l.rsc.6
Nov 15	George Judge	London	l.pts.8
Nov 28	Rudy Edwards	Carmarthen	w.rsc.5
Dec 6	Al McCarthy	Wembley	l.rsc.7

1961

Mar 6	Junior Cassidy	Maesteg	w.dis.7
Jun 21	Paddy Kelly	Cardiff	w.rsc.6
Jul 11	Danny O`Brien	Wembley	l.rsc.6

Gordon Blakey

Chapter 11

Harry Carroll started to box at the age of nine and was a member of the Splott YMCA club. Here he came under the guidance of Ernie Hurford who looked after him through both his amateur and professional career. This turned out to be the perfect partnership for Harry and his respect for his old mentor still shines through as in conversation he still refers to him as Mr Hurford. As an amateur Harry took part in over 200 contests, losing only six and his gym mates as a youngster included Dai Merchant, Terry Gooding and Dai Furnish. As a young boy he was badly burned and was always unable to properly close his right fist. During a distinguished amateur career he represented Wales at international level and his team mates included "Ponty" Davies, Howard Winstone, Malcolm Collins, Brian Curvis, Don Sainsbury and Roger Pleece, an unbelievably talented combination of boxers.

During the 1958 Empire Games, which were held in Cardiff, Harry fondly remembers sparring with members of the Australian boxing team at England's gym and he was able to pass on news of their strengths and weaknesses to members of the Welsh team.

Southpaw Harry turned professional with Benny Jacobs in 1958 and in a career that lasted six and a half years he was only beaten once in twentyfive contests, the defeat coming at the hands of Howard Winstone, who ironically, had also suffered a career threatening injury when he lost the tips of three fingers on his right hand in a factory accident.

Harry honed his skills in the gym sparring with Darkie Hughes, Teddy Best, who was dangerous with his left hook and his head and would always treat a sparring session like a fight, Ponty Davies, Gordon Blakey and even Joe Erskine. These names reflect the quality of preparation all these boxers enjoyed and it certainly prepared them for the rigours of the ring.

He made his debut at Birmingham on April 3rd, 1958 and knocked out fellow-debutant Phil Hall in the first round. Just three weeks later he was back in action in Cardiff when he knocked out Dave Board in the third round. In June, he beat Chris Elliott on points over six rounds in London and in July he stopped Levi John in the second round at Coney Beach Arena, Porthcawl. Top of the bill was Dick Richardson against the American Bob Baker with Dick taking the decision on points over ten rounds.

Harry had made an outstanding start to his professional career and he rounded off the year by stopping Jimmy Fitzpatrick in two rounds at the National

Sporting Club but chest problems were about to force him out of the ring for a year. He was sent to see Dr Jack Matthews, the former Welsh rugby international at one of the Cardiff hospitals and a heart murmur was suspected. Dr Jack had enjoyed his own moment of boxing glory when he boxed Rocky Marciano in 1944 at RAF St. Athan, several years before the "Brockton Blockbuster" would wreak havoc in the heavyweight division. Harry`s condition needed to be monitored over a period of time and his return to the ring came almost exactly a year later.

He only boxed twice in 1959 with both contests taking place in December. He knocked out Dave Ford in the third round at Manor Place Baths and then stopped Russ Waddon in five rounds at Cheltenham. Harry was being astutely matched but was already making quite an impression in the featherweight division.

His first contest in 1960 saw him in action against a more experienced opponent. Tommy Williams had already had fifteen contests but Harry was on a roll and stopped him in the fifth round of their contest in Cardiff. In March, he faced Chris Elliott again. By now, Elliott had notched up twentythree contests and Harry had to travel all eight rounds to claim a points decision.

Five more contests followed that year and all ended inside the distance, such was the power of Harry`s punching. He boxed in Cardiff, Merthyr, Aberdare and Porthcawl. The bill at Aberdare featured Howard Winstone against Sergio Milan and Harry`s stablemate Ron "Ponty" Davies beating Scot Frankie Jones on points over ten rounds. Harry was in devastating form knocking out Hugh Dougherty in the fourth round.

At Porthcawl, Harry stopped Andy Hayford in the third round, but fight fans will always remember the night of August 29th for the fight after the fight! Dick Richardson had won the European Heavyweight Championship in Dortmund by stopping Hans Kalbfell in the thirteenth round. He was now making his first defence of his title against Brian London of Blackpool. It had been a bad-tempered affair, but all hell was let loose after London retired at the end of the eighth round as the respective cornermen became involved in a punch-up.

As 1961 dawned Harry had notched up fourteen contests and only one of them had lasted the distance but this was about to change as all four contests of the year were to last the full course. In his first contest he was held to a draw over eight rounds by Hugh O`Neill at Sophia Gardens, Cardiff but then came two more contests against Chris Elliott with Harry winning both eight-round contests on points. In all, they boxed four times and each one resulted in a points victory for the Cardiff man. In October he beat Paddy Read on points over ten rounds in Cardiff.

Harry was still being plagued by chest problems and during his career he also damaged a hand which needed a bone graft but Benny made sure he quickly got the best of attention and also paid the bill for the operation which ran to £350. There are countless stories of Benny`s generosity in such circumstances and his care and concern for his boxers is beyond question.

By now there was talk of an all-Welsh title fight with Howard Winstone having taken the British Featherweight Championship from Terry Spinks.

Harry possessed a spearing right hand and was a heavy hitter. He moved well in the ring and was sound defensively while rarely taking a backward step. All in all, he was a dangerous opponent for the young champion, and after Howard had defended successfully against Derry Treanor at Wembley the potentially explosive match was made for Maindy Stadium on May 30th, with local promoter Stan Cottle securing the contest for the Welsh capital.

I still have vivid memories of this particular early summer evening as it was the first British Title fight for me to attend and it was my first meeting with both Jack Petersen and Tommy Farr. As darkness came and fight-time approached, the lights went down in preparation for Howard and Harry to make their way to the ring. Firstly, Harry was picked out by the spotlight and made his way to the ring to the sound of the Jack Solomons fanfare which always added that indefinable touch to a special occasion, while Benny followed closely with his white towel characteristically draped over his shoulder.

Next it was Howard`s turn to make his way to the ring in similar fashion as he and Eddie Thomas seemed enclosed in that pool of light. I was fourteen at the time but would be forever hooked on the atmosphere and excitement of big-fight night. There has never been anything quite like it for me.

The cheering of about 10,000 fans provided the backdrop for the fighters to go to work and success would give Howard outright ownership of the Lonsdale Belt, the first Welshman to win a belt in the featherweight division since Jim Driscoll.

Howard gave a superb exhibition of boxing though at times during the contest he showed his liking for a fight and did tend to lunge at his opponent occasionally. Beforehand, I felt that Harry`s punching power would have been a significant element in the contest but Winstone was in the mood for a masterclass and Harry needed all his courage to withstand the attacks of the Merthyr man.

Howard allowed Harry to lead but would then punish him with head shots and after six rounds the accumulative effect of Howard`s impeccably accurate punches was plain for all to see.

The first round was fought at a hectic pace and as early as the second round Harry`s right eye began to swell. Subsequently, his nose began to bleed and as the rounds passed Harry picked up more facial damage. At the end of the sixth round, Benny took one look at his fighter as he returned to the corner and realised that any further work on the injuries would be useless and he called over referee Harry Gibbs to indicate their retirement.

And so, Harry`s title dreams were over. In the past he had almost always been able to dominate his opponent, but on this occasion, even though he was the bigger man and the taller man he was unable to match the speed and versatility of Howard`s work and Boxing News summed up the contest as follows: "Time and time again Winstone`s combinations hammered Carroll round the ring and reduced him to stumbling helplessness, though there was never any danger of his going down"

Harry was not the first boxer, and would certainly not be the last to suffer such a comprehensive defeat at the hands of Howard, but a defeat like this can take time to get over and the result was that Harry was out of the ring for a year.

He returned to action almost exactly a year later having decided to move up to lightweight and stopped Tony Icke in the eighth round of their contest at the National Sporting Club, and in July , he was held to a draw over eight rounds in Cardiff by Jim "Spike" McCormack. In some ways this was a frustrating contest for Harry. He hurt McCormack early in the contest with a combination which immediately sent the Irishman into retreat mode and he spent the remainder of the contest trying to avoid Harry's powerful punches.

In January, 1964 he faced Brian Brazier at Olympia and stopped his man in the sixth round. This bill featured Howard Winstone against the American, Don Johnson with referee Jack Hart finding controversially in the American's favour after ten rounds while jointly topping the bill was Billy Walker against Joe Bygraves.

Brazier was formerly a dual ABA Champion at Lightwelterweight but weighed in at 9st 11lbs, as indeed did Harry, for their contest. It was a pulsating battle with Harry winning on a stoppage because of a cut eye in the sixth round.

Brazier, usually the skilful boxer, waded into Harry and was prepared to trade punches. In the second round, his tactics almost paid off when he floored Harry for a count of nine. He concentrated on body shots and was having to take a good deal of punishment himself in return, but in the third round Harry fought back with great determination and his exceptional footwork made Brazier miss wildly.

The fighters stood toe to toe in the fourth round and the crowd applauded almost throughout the round while in the fifth round, Brazier began to feel the pace and Carroll scored heavily to the body.

Both boxers were showing signs of tiredness in the sixth but the crowd cheered wildly as they both ignored defence, but then, Brazier suffered a cut over his right eye and sadly, the referee had to intervene.

Harry was back in action less than a fortnight later on a show promoted by Phil Edwards at the Drill Hall in Cardiff and he stopped Peter Lavery in the eighth round of their contest with several of his stablemates also in action.

He was back at the Drill Hall in May, once more with his old friend Phil Edwards promoting. This time Harry faced the tried and tested Jamaican Con Mount Bassie in an eight rounder at lightweight. It seemed that this would be a battle where the key elements would be Harry's right hand and the Jamaican's in-fighting. Con would be bringing huge experience to the ring but Harry too brought power coupled with superb attacking and defensive skills. On paper, the match had everything and Harry took the decision on points proving that he was still one of the most dangerous men in Britain in the lighter weight divisions.

Harry sustained a cut over his right eye in the third round, but in the words of Boxing News "soundly outpointed his durable opponent in this exciting eight-rounder" with the report of the contest running as follows: "The fight had a lively, heavy-punching start that promised fireworks all the way until, early in the third, the crowd groaned as cut-prone Carroll's eye was cut and referee Ike Powell stepped in to take a close look at the injury.

Satisfied for the moment, Ike waved the fight on and Bassie sprang forward to pile on the pressure towards the quick end which now seemed certain.

Fortunately for Carroll, he showed as much intelligence in defence as he had a few seconds ago in non-stop attack, and for the rest of the fight he set a peek-a-boo, keep away pattern that turned the bull-like Bassie into a classic portrait of frustration.

At the end of every round, however, Carroll`s corner had to patch up that troublesome eye again, and at times it was touch and go whether this, after all his guile and skill, would decide the issue.

Bassie, twice warned for using his head, seemed to be progressively forgetting his greater experience as the rounds slipped by—his one aim was to close in on Carroll and mix it, a fading hope that drove him wild.

Southpaw Harry`s quick rights were building up a wide lead, and we wonder if even he was surprised at this turn of events after being forced to change his tactics in the third—before which the fight was even.

The final, decisive pay-off for Carroll came in the last round when his chopping left decked Bassie. Though the Jamaican got up before the count could start, you can count on one hand the number of times he has hit the canvas in his long career.

Rounds seven and eight were clearly Carroll`s and even though Bassie`s great strength never allowed the fight to be one-sided for long, there was no possible alternative to the verdict".

On October 5th, he was matched with Mickey Laud from St. Ives at the Lyceum Ballroom in the Strand and this turned out to be Harry`s final contest. Mickey was a solid professional who came to Merthyr regularly as one of Howard Winstone`s sparring partners and his record stood at ten wins, three losses and two draws but Harry emerged as the winner on points over eight rounds.

The charity show was staged by promoter Harry Grossmith with the proceeds going to the widow of Welsh boxer Lyn James who sadly died following a contest at Shoreditch in June. Lyn was a young featherweight protégé of former Welsh Middleweight Champion Glen Moody from Pontypridd. Topping the bill was Hoxton`s Vic Andreetti against John White of Chicago with the Londoner winning on points. Also on the bill was one of Harry`s former opponents, namely, Chris Elliott who lost on points to Peter Cheevers. Harry, now weighing a fraction over 9st 9lbs took a close decision over his heavier opponent.

In an all-southpaw battle, the speed of Harry`s right hand was the telling factor and in the words of Boxing News he was "just too classy for his gallant rival".

Mickey Laud came forward throughout the fight throwing both hands and trying to bustle Harry out of his stride, thus making the last three rounds close, but at the final bell he had to acknowledge that Harry was the superior fighter.

And so the plush surroundings of the Lyceum Ballroom provided the backdrop for Harry`s final appearance in the ring and the fact that he was "just too classy for his gallant rival" nicely sums up much of his career. He was indeed a class act, blessed with skills in both defence and attack and as many of his opponents would testify, he could punch.

Harry was to have faced Maurice Cullen on the road to the British Lightweight title and had travelled to Durham the day before the contest only to learn that the fight was off. Having trained hard for the contest he was absolutely ready to go and found the disappointment of missing out on this contest difficult to handle. He became disillusioned with the sport and decided it was time to retire.

After retiring he played rugby for about two years and began to train young boxers. One of his undoubted success stories was David Griffiths who won the Welsh title at Lightwelterweight in 1982, 83, and 84. David also won the ABA title in 1984 and represented Britain at the Olympic Games at Los Angeles the same year, and this, for Harry was one of the highlights of their partnership.

David made his professional debut on the undercard of the contest between Don Curry and Colin Jones for the WBA Welterweight Title at the NEC in Birmingham on January 19th, 1985 where he stopped George Jones in the second round. I had the pleasure of refereeing his third contest at the Star Leisure Centre in Splott, Cardiff when he stopped Les Remikie after four rounds. He won the Welsh Lightwelterweight Title beating Cardiff's Mark Pearce on points and the rematch ended in the same way, but following a stoppage defeat to Dave Pierre at the Café Royal in February 1990 he retired from the sport.

As a trainer, Harry undoubtedly had the recipe, but sadly for the sport, when he began to look after boxers in the professional code, he had to relinquish his amateur licences.

In more recent years Harry has been a member of the Welsh Area Council and for a time he was Chief Inspector. Unfortunately, he had to step down from this position because of health problems but he remains involved as a council member where his experience and knowledge of the game is of enormous value.

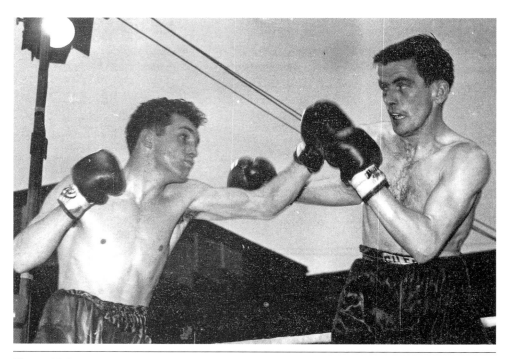

Howard Winstone (left) & Harry Carroll.
pic: Courtesy of Western Mail

Harry Carroll

Featherweight
Cardiff
Born: September 22nd , 1939

1958

Apr 3	Phil Hall	Birmingham	w.ko.1
Apr 23	Dave Board	Cardiff	w.ko.3
Jun 11	Chris Elliott	London	w.pts.6
Jul 9	Levi John	Coney Beach	w.rsc.2
Dec 29	Jimmy Fitzpatrick	NSC	w.rsc.2

1959

Dec 8	Dave Ford	Manor Place Baths	w.ko.3
Dec 14	Russ Waddon	Cheltenham	w.rsc.5

1960

Jan 14	Tommy Williams	Cardiff	w.rsc.5
Mar 21	Chris Elliott	Derby	w.pts.8
Mar 31	Nye Ankrah	Cardiff	w.rsc.2
Jun 14	John Smillie	Merthyr	w.rsc.2
Aug 15	Hugh Dougherty	Aberdare	w.ko.4
Aug 29	Andy Hayford	Coney Beach	w.rsc.3
Nov 24	John Bacon	Cardiff	w.ko.5

1961

Jan 19	Hugh O`Neill	Cardiff	d.pts.8
Apr 7	Chris Elliott	Leicester	w.pts.8
May 12	Chris Elliott	Manchester	w.pts.8
Oct 25	Paddy Read	Cardiff	w.pts.10

1962

May 30	Howard Winstone	Maindy Stadium	l.rtd.6
	(British Featherweight Title)		

1963

May 15	Tony Icke	NSC	w.rsc.8
Jul 29	Jim Spike McCormack	Cardiff	d.pts.8

1964

Jan 28	Brian Brazier	Olympia	w.rsc.6
Feb 10	Peter Lavery	Cardiff	w.rsc.8
May 4	Con Mount Bassie	Cardiff	w.pts.8
Oct 5	Mickey Laud	London	w.pts.8

Harry Carroll

Chapter 12

Tanos Lambrianides came to Wales as the ex-welterweight champion of Greece and turned professional with Benny Jacobs. He made his professional debut on February 4th, 1959 on a bill at Sophia Gardens Pavilion topped by Phil Edwards against Martin Hansen. Tanos, a twentythree-year old marine engineer weighed-in at 10st. 7. 1/2lbs while his opponent, Gus Harry from Trinidad came in 3lbs lighter.

Curiously, because of an order from the "Ministry of Labour", as the Department of Employment was then known, Tanos was required to donate his purse money to charity, but although he was in effect fighting for nothing, he turned on the style and won impressively on points over six rounds.

Tanos lost his second contest on points to Peter Anderson in London but he was fit, powerful and dangerous. He was in action again on May 27th, in Cardiff and on a bill topped by Phil Edwards against Michel Diouf he forced Tommy Hayes to retire in the third round and this marked the beginning of a ten-fight unbeaten run when he stopped the likes of Steve Richards and Joe Sommerville.

His run of success came to an end on May 9th, 1960 when he lost on points over eight rounds to Boswell St. Louis at the Royal Albert Hall.

He returned to winning ways with a points win over Eddie Phillips and a two round stoppage of Jimmy Lawson at Porthcawl in August. He was then matched with Mick Leahy at Wembley. On the same bill, promoted by Jack Solomons, Brian Curvis stopped the American Johnny Gorman in the ninth round while Henry Cooper damaged a hand in his points win over the Texan Roy Harris.

Brian Curvis was far from his best while Cooper's opponent was poor and the crowd needed something to stir interest. This was provided when Tanos caused the upset of the night by outpointing Leahy over eight rounds.

The Irishman had beaten the Australian, George Barnes and Boswell St. Louis but he could not match the ferocity of Lambrianides and by the end, there were many fans who felt that with continued improvement, he could give Brian Curvis a serious test.

Sadly, two fights later, things started to go badly wrong for Tanos when, on November 16th, he was knocked out by Boswell St. Louis at King's Lynn. Barely a week later he was awarded a draw by referee Joe Morgan against Al Sharp, of Belfast. Ringsiders were surprised by the decision but the referee must have felt that the Greek was the more aggressive of the two though Sharp must have scored heavily with his accurate left hand work. Tanos kept attacking up to the final bell but was constantly caught by Sharp's accurate head shots.

Tanos boxed just three times during 1961, losing a rematch with Mick Leahy on points over eight rounds at Liverpool.

On May 30th, he appeared at Wembley on the night when John Caldwell won the world title against Alphonse Halimi. Tanos faced Tony Mancini, the Southern Area Welterweight Champion, and lost on points after eight rounds. The rounds followed a similar pattern with Tanos going forward with his head down and his fists held high, swinging away with both hands, but Mancini would just step out of the way and pick his man off with precision left-hand work.

After losing to Johnny Kramer in July at Wembley he was out of the ring until February, 1962. He came back with a stoppage win over Ronnie Rush at Maesteg but that was his final win. On April 17th, he lost on points to former British Champion, Wally Swift at the Granby Halls, Leicester. He showed aggression throughout and was prepared to trade punches, but he was unable to cope with Swift's piercing left hand. Tanos swayed, bobbed and weaved but Swift was so accurate. Tanos was more effective in the clinches and occasionally got through but Swift was able to tie him up when the need arose.

In the third round Tanos shook Swift with a powerful left hook but generally, Wally held on and was able to negate his work and soon recovered to score heavily with those precise left hands to the head.

Lambrianides tried to force the fight during the final two rounds, but time and again he ran into the left hand of Swift, who, it should be remembered, had given Brian Curvis two hard fights.

In June, Tanos travelled to Cagliari and was stopped in the fourth round against Fortunato Manca and following a defeat at the hands of Jimmy McGrail later in the year he decided to retire perhaps without fulfilling his early promise.

Tanos Lambrianides

Welterweight
Born: Greece September 1st, 1933

1959

Feb 4	Gus Harry	Cardiff	w.pts.6
Mar 24	Peter Anderson	London	l.pts.6
May 27	Tommy Hayes	Cardiff	w.rtd.3
Jul 7	Steve Richards	London	w.rsc.2
Sep 1	Mike Robbins	London	w.rsc.6
Oct 28	Tony Valledy	Cardiff	w.rtd.4
Nov 10	Harry Haydock	London	w.rsc.2
Dec 8	Mike Robbins	London	w.pts.8

1960

Jan 19	Peter Cobblah	London	w.pts.8
Feb 9	Joe Sommerville	London	w.rsc.2
Mar 31	Barry Burke	Cardiff	w.dis.2
May 9	Gordon Enoch	Swansea	w.pts.8
Jun 21	Boswell St Louis	London	l.pts.8
Aug 19	Eddie Phillips	Banbury	w.pts.6
Aug 29	Jimmy Lawson	Porthcawl	w.rsc.2
Sep 13	Mick Leahy	Wembley	w.pts.8
Oct 10	Sani Armstrong	Manchester	w.rtd.7
Nov 16	Boswell St Louis	King`s Lynn	l.ko.3
Nov 24	Al Sharpe	Cardiff	d.8

1961

Apr 20	Mick Leahy	Liverpool	l.pts.8
May 30	Tony Mancini	Wembley	l.pts.8
Jul 11	Johnny Kramer	Wembley	l.pts.8

1962

Feb 12	Ronnie Rush	Maesteg	w.rsc.6
Apr 17	Wally Swift	Leicester	l.pts.8
Jun 2	Fortunato Manca	Cagliari	l.rsc.4
Oct 9	Jimmy McGrail	London	l.pts.10

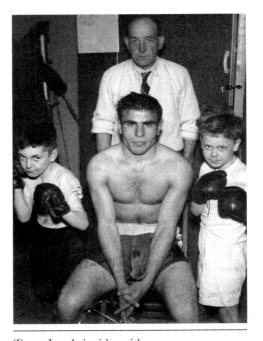

Tanos Lambrianides with
trainer Ernie Hurford.
pic: The Collection of Dave Furnish

Chapter 13

Terry Crimmins enjoyed a successful amateur career representing Wales at international level and, representing Vale ABC he won the Welsh ABA Bantamweight title in 1959 by outpointing Dai Corp (Victoria Park) in the final. When he turned professional he was looked after by Jackie Sutton before joining Benny's stable. He was a tough, uncompromising fighter who was strong on the inside and many fighters would testify to the quality of his body punching.

He made his debut at the age of eighteen on a show at Colwyn Bay which was promoted by Arthur Hughes, the former Blackpool, Wrexham and Wales centre-half. The bill featured several of Benny's boys and Terry began in style, knocking out his opponent Mark Quinn of London in the second round with a perfect left-hook.

From August to December, 1959 he engaged in six contests losing just one when he retired in the second round of his fight against Bill Downer.

During 1960, he boxed eight times and again there was just one loss when he was disqualified for a low blow in the third round of his contest against Don Weller at Aberdare. This was Weller's sixth contest and in his next appearance Don captured the Southern Area Bantamweight title at the National Sporting Club with a win on points over twelve rounds against Dennis East thus establishing his calibre. In November, Terry beat Tommy Burgoyne on points in Cardiff in a memorable "nobbins" battle.

Terry floored his opponent early in the contest, but such was the courage of Burgoyne that as the contest progressed he gave Terry a great deal of trouble. They continued punching toe to toe right up to the end of the contest and it was the Cardiff man's toughest assignment to date, but the final bell brought a shower of "nobbins" from the crowd and in a typical gesture of generosity, Benny announced that the money would be donated to the Six Bells Colliery Disaster Fund.

He remained undefeated through 1961 and started by stopping Tommy Burgoyne in the seventh round of their rematch in Cardiff but perhaps the most sensational result of the year came on June 21st, when Terry, having his seventeenth contest, stopped Len "Luggie" Reece in the sixth round at Cardiff.

Reece, in his twenty-eighth contest brought a wealth of experience to the ring. In 1957 he had challenged Frankie Jones for the British and Commonwealth Flyweight titles vacated by Dai Dower, but was knocked out in the eleventh round of their contest at Porthcawl. He went on to face Billy Rafferty, Ronnie Davies and George Bowes and in 1959 he lost on points again to Rafferty at the Kelvin Hall in Glasgow in an eliminator for the British Bantamweight title.

Crimmins weighed in for their contest at 8st. 8.lbs with Len coming in half a pound heavier. This was undoubtedly Terry`s most outstanding success to date.

Reece, with his clever counterpunching took the first three rounds but gradually the strength of Crimmins became the crucial factor. Terry used his strength to get inside where he worked away effectively. In the fateful sixth round he caught Reece with a superb left-hook to the chin and Reece fell into the arms of the referee. He was clearly out, and the referee had no alternative but to stop the contest.

After forcing George O`Neill to retire in five rounds at Maesteg, Terry faced the Venezuelan Nelson Estrada over ten rounds at Sophia Gardens. Estrada was an experienced performer having beaten Ignacio Pina, who had beaten Irishman Freddie Gilroy, but he had not reckoned on the courage of Crimmins, who seemed to enjoy a contest as it increased in intensity. Alan Wood, writing in the Western Mail described the fight as one of the most convincing wins of his career. Terry was clearly maturing and used his left jab well with the right hand held close. Crimmins boxed in a cool, unruffled manner throughout, while Estrada tried in vain to disrupt the Cardiff man`s plans.

Terry was content to jab away from the first bell, blocking the counters of Estrada and using his right sparingly. Terry`s jab was rarely out of his opponent`s face while Estrada only scored with the occasional right as Crimmins dropped his left after leading.

By the fourth round Estrada clearly wanted Terry to come in close, but Crimmins did not allow himself to be drawn in, though in the last two rounds he used more of his right hand to seal his points victory.

On May 30th, 1962, Terry faced Don Weller in a rematch on the undercard of the contest between Howard Winstone and Harry Carroll at Maindy Stadium. This time, Crimmins avenged his earlier defeat with a convincing points win over eight rounds.

Terry was masterful from the outset and Weller looked demoralised long before the final bell. The win lifted Terry to third place in the British bantamweight rankings with champion Freddie Gilroy due to defend his title against John Caldwell, the man they described as the "Cold Eyed Killer" in October in Belfast. This subsequently turned out to be one of the great fights with Caldwell forced to retire in the ninth round.

Earlier that month, Terry returned to the ring to face Brian Cartwright, having been out of action since May with a leg injury. At the Drill Hall in Cardiff, Crimmins started slowly and endured some uncomfortable moments during the first three rounds but gradually his left jab, coupled with excellent movement about the ring, began to have its effect though he was caught at times with a right counter, when again, he would drop his left after leading.

Cartwright began to tire from the effects of Terry`s body punching and Crimmins was well on top in rounds five and six. Despite some desperate right hands from Cartwright, Crimmins forced his man to the ropes and was punishing him with both hands when the referee intervened in the seventh round.

In March, 1963, Terry faced Freddie Dobson of Manchester on the undercard of the contest between Henry Cooper and Dick Richardson at Wembley. Dick was knocked out in the fifth round, but Terry, having his first fight at featherweight, forced Dobson to retire at the end of the seventh round. Crimmins had been inactive for a few months but had been sparring with Howard Winstone, who had himself beaten Dobson in four rounds some months earlier. Terry took a little time to warm up, but eventually found his rhythm with the jab and his powerful counters, and by the sixth round he was attacking Dobson with both hands.

In the seventh round, Dobson was floored for a count of six. The bell interrupted the count, but by this time Dobson was too exhausted to continue and had to retire.

Terry Crimmins then decided to go to Australia for a few months and on June 7th, he was stopped by Kid Oliva in the third round at Melbourne. He was back in action five weeks later and beat Gilberto Brondi on points over twelve rounds, but unbelievably, on August 9th, Brondi stopped him in the first round and this was a crushing disappointment.

During his time in Australia he began to put on weight and subsequently had great difficulty in reducing. On his return he was inactive during 1964 and was becoming disillusioned with the sport.

Terry returned to action on April 12th, 1965 at the National Sporting Club where he faced Bobby Davies of West Ham. For his last fight in Australia Terry was virtually boxing at lightweight, but he was now back to featherweight and showed something of his old skill in a decisive points win. The accurate left hand work of Crimmins bemused the powerfully built Londoner who did manage to connect with some looping punches, but whose work was effectively smothered by the clever Welshman. Terry frequently boxed on the retreat but his skills were too much for Davies who was nevertheless a top-ten fighter.

After drawing against John McDermott at the National Sporting Club, Terry`s final contest was a rematch against Brian Cartwright. Topping the bill at Birmingham City`s football ground was the contest between Henry Cooper and Johnny Prescott. Terry, unfortunately, lost on points over eight rounds and this proved to be his final appearance in the ring.

It seems clear that Terry Crimmins had not enjoyed the smoothest of relationships with Benny and at times felt that he was not getting the publicity he deserved. Terry tended to keep himself to himself but would always speak his mind, and sadly, this approach does not always please people. Dai Corp tells of their sparring sessions and how they did their roadwork together, with neither of them being too keen on this aspect of their preparation, though he was superb in sparring and was capable of causing problems even for Howard Winstone for about four rounds, by which time the skill and strength of Winstone would begin to have its effect.

During the early 1960s the Bantamweight division in Britain was extremely strong and at one time Dai Corp and Terry Crimmins were both highly placed in the top ten with Freddie Gilroy and John Caldwell above them and with Billy Rafferty and George Bowes also in the frame, but in assessing Terry`s career one cannot help feeling that for a boxer so skilful, strong and aggressive maybe he never quite fulfilled his potential in the paid ranks.

Terry Crimmins

Bantamweight
Cardiff
Born: September 28th, 1940
Died July, 2004
Welsh ABA Bantamweight Champion, 1959

1959

Aug 22	Mark Quinn	Colwyn Bay	w.ko.2
Sep 1	Micky Redmond	Aberdare	w.rsc.2
Oct 28	Bill Downer	Cardiff	l.rtd.2
Nov 23	Pete Hallberg	Banbury	w.pts.6
Dec 2	Teddy Tyrrell	Liverpool	w.rsc.6
Dec 14	James Barlow	Cheltenham	w.pts.6

1960

Jan 25	Russ Hawkeswell	Coventry	w.pts.6
Feb 2	Steve Regan	Walsall	w.rsc.3
Feb 9	Don Cosheril	London	w.pts.6
Jul 5	Johnny Lewis	Wembley	w.pts.6
Aug 15	Don Weller	Aberdare	l.dis.3
Sep 22	Eddie O`Connor	Cardiff	w.rsc.6
Nov 24	Tommy Burgoyne	Cardiff	w.pts.6
Dec 6	Don Cosheril	Wembley	w.pts.8

1961

Jan 19	Tommy Burgoyne	Cardiff	w.rsc.7
May 29	Johnny O`Callaghan	London	w.rsc.6
Jun 21	Len Reece	Cardiff	w.rsc.6
Sep 11	Hugh Riley	Cardiff	w.ko.2
Oct 3	George O`Neill	Maesteg	w.rtd.5
Oct 25	Nel Estrada	Cardiff	w.pts.10

1962

May 15	Dele Majeke	Maesteg	w.pts.8
May 30	Don Weller	Cardiff	w.pts.8
Oct 1	Brian Cartwright	Cardiff	w.rsc.7

1963

Mar 26	Freddie Dobson	Wembley	w.rtd.7
Jun 7	Kid Oliva	Melbourne	l.rsc.3
Jul 12	Gilberto Brondi	Melbourne	w.pts.12
Aug 9	Gilberto Brondi	Melbourne	l.rsc.1

1964

	Inactive

1965

Apr 12	Bobby Davis	London	w.pts.8
May 3	John McDermott	London	d.8
Jun 15	Brian Cartwright	Birmingham	l.pts.8

Terry Crimmins
pic: Courtesy of Gordon Blakey

Chapter 14

As a young boy starting out in the sport of boxing Lennie "The Lion" Williams was looked after by Verdun Thomas in a small gym at Nantyffyllon. After about two years his trainer suggested a move to the gym at Caerau where he would have better opportunities for sparring and where he was guided by Dai Jenkins, a man in his eighties who was very much "old school" according to Lennie and feared by the boys in the gym. Lennie remembers him as an extremely good cornerman who was always able to hand out the correct tactical advice because of the careful way in which he watched opponents working.

Even before leaving school at the age of fifteen, Lennie used to spend time during the school holidays working out at Benny`s gym in Customhouse Street. He would be booked in at the Linden Court Hotel in Newport Road at Benny`s expense and would catch the trolley-bus in to town each morning. On the bus he would invariably meet trainer Ernie Hurford and when they reached the gym a group would set off on their roadwork with Benny following behind in his Bedford transit. Already the young "Lion" was doing his roadwork in the company of Phil Edwards, Joe Erskine, Harry Carroll, Teddy Best, Darkie Hughes and Terry Crimmins. He was also allowed to spar with them all with the exception of Harry Carroll and Teddy Best, who could never resist the temptation to let go with his fierce left-hook, though Lennie freely admits that Phil and Joe would never throw hurtful punches in return. He particularly enjoyed his sparring sessions with Johnny Thomas, Terry Crimmins and Aryee Jackson who he rated highly as a boxer but whose style resembled a human windmill.

Lennie represented Wales as a schoolboy and won the Class A Welsh Junior title at eight stone in 1960. He also took the ABA Junior Title at the same weight but then decided to turn professional and had his first contest on January 19th, 1961 at the age of sixteen having first been spotted by Benny Jacobs at the age of twelve when winning a contest at Ogmore Vale. Welsh fight fans eagerly awaited his professional debut and it came at Sophia Gardens, Cardiff on a show jointly promoted by Syd Wignall and Jack Solomons and featured Howard Winstone against Empire Featherweight Champion Floyd Robertson topping the bill in an international ten round contest. Also on the bill were Lennie`s stablemates Harry Carroll and Terry Crimmins while Merthyr`s Don James was matched with Alex O`Neill from Belfast. Vince Brown and Jim Slattery completed the bill and they could always be relied upon to entertain the crowd. Lennie`s first opponent in the professional ranks was to have been the experienced Dave Board from Taunton but on the night he faced Steve Regan who was duly stopped inside a round. A month later, Lennie was in the ring again at Wolverhampton where he knocked out Chris Dodds in the first round and his third contest saw him on home ground where he stopped Bobby Fiddes in the third round at Maesteg.

In all, Lennie boxed thirteen times during his first year in the professional ranks and boxed twice a month in September, October and November building up momentum and a great body of support. His workload ensured valuable experience and guaranteed a good level of fitness. He was able to earn steadily and his army of fans were guaranteed excitement each time he climbed into the ring.

Outside the ring, Lennie worked as a colliery blacksmith in the Llynfi Valley and this undoubtedly contributed to his strength in much the same way as it had for Eric Boon and Bob Fitzsimmons to name but two who were similarly employed. His father was a miner who also boxed as a welterweight and as with so many fighters in the valleys of South Wales, a background in mining often provided the raw ingredients for success in the roped square, but Lennie`s other passion was horse riding and he frequently rode at point to point meetings. Lennie tells a story of riding at Penybont races in August 1963. Shortly before he was due to ride Benny turned up in the company of Mickey Duff and Mike Barrett in an attempt to persuade Lennie not to ride because they feared he might be injured, but they had not reckoned on Lennie`s passion for riding and he went ahead with his ride. Continuing the family tradition here, when Lennie himself became a father, his son Tyrone eventually went on to become a highly successful jockey.

An early opportunity to taste the big time came on July 11th, 1961, when he boxed Norman Swales at Wembley on the undercard of the contest between Terry Downes and Paul Pender for the Middleweight Championship of the World. The colourful Downes achieved his ambition by forcing Pender to retire after nine rounds of a contest handled by Welsh referee Ike Powell and Lennie made short work of Swales, stopping him in the first round. Already, his opponents were finding it difficult to cope with his punching power and Billy Williams, the durable bantam from Cannock Chase became only the second opponent of the year to take Lennie to a points decision, the first having been Gerry Jones who was subsequently knocked out in the first round of their rematch.

During 1962 Lennie boxed on twelve occasions and again many of these contests were very close together. His first eight-rounder was against Frank Lannion at Maesteg, Lannion retiring in the fifth round and in his next contest he stopped Jack Dillon in two rounds at the Seymour Hall in what was his first bill-topping appearance. A damaged hand sustained in his win over Billy Williams kept the "Lion" out of the ring until June, when he returned to beat George O`Neill in two rounds at Corwen. O`Neill, a veteran from Belfast was taken completely out of his stride with the Welshman flooring him twice in the first round, both for counts of nine. Only three contests went the distance, his last two contests of the year resulting in wins on points over eight rounds, the former against Al Rocca and the latter against Tommy Atkins at Blackpool. He rounded off his training for the Al Rocca contest at Joe Bloom`s gym in London where Sugar Ray Robinson was preparing for his contest against Terry Downes at Wembley. Many fans gathered at the gym to see the legend at work and Lennie claims to have been mesmerised by his skipping routine as Ray`s trainer constantly whistled the tune of "Sweet Georgia Brown". During his stay, Ray, true to form, turned up at the gym immaculately dressed and this left an indelible impression on the minds of those present.

Already, television audiences were beginning to appreciate this exciting young fighter and there were interesting offers from Canadian and American promoters and it is worth noting that the British Boxing Board of Control was already having to vet prospective opponents, such was the impression he was making. Lennie was blasting his way through the featherweight division but his power was coupled with uncanny anticipation, elusiveness and an almost fierce self-belief and as 1963 dawned he was unbeaten in twentyfive contests. Having said that, he hit the canvas for the first time when he beat Billy Evans of St Helens in a contest at Wolverhampton before coming through to win convincingly on points.

On January 22nd , 1963 he was matched with Dele Majeke at Smethwick and he knocked his opponent out in the second round. Pressure was mounting for a match against Frankie "The Tiger" Taylor from Lancaster and the press were quick to build the contest using the "Lion" versus the "Tiger" angle. Both were showcased at Olympia on January 29th when Lennie knocked out Jimmy Carson in the second round while Frankie stopped Jean Leroux in the first round.

On the same bill, Brian London beat the tough American Tom McNeeley who had previously challenged Floyd Patterson for the Heavyweight Championship of the World. After a rough start London settled for a points win and there was more heavyweight interest when West Ham`s Blond Bomber Billy Walker scored a controversial second round knockout over the experienced Peter Bates.

Benny never missed an opportunity to stoke up interest in his fighters and in Lennie he knew he had something special. He was excited by his young charge and stated: "He`s colourful, confident, a smart boxer, unpredictable, a real character and one of the very few- maybe the only one in Britain right now- who can put a man away with one punch".

The match against Frankie Taylor was set for April 9th at the Royal Albert Hall with Mike Barrett promoting one of his first major contests. Frankie had enjoyed a successful amateur career winning the ABA Bantamweight title in 1960 and winning a gold medal at featherweight in 1961 at the European Championships held in Belgrade but one of the highlights of his career was representing Great Britain in the team which beat the United States 10-0 at Wembley in November of the same year with Taylor beating his man in three rounds. He turned professional with Bobby Neill, the former British Featherweight Champion who featured in two fierce battles with Terry Spinks and he was unbeaten as a professional when he came face to face with Lennie. Both boxers enjoyed huge support from their loyal fans and it was clear that something would have to give!

It is worth noting that at the time of the contest, Taylor had only just broken into the ratings and Lennie was not in the top ten, but such was the strength of the featherweight division at the time in Britain and the level of interest ensured that the contest was a sell-out weeks in advance.

The report in Boxing News ran as follows: "Nineteen-year-old Williams… committed the common error among youngsters of failing to pace himself properly.

He raced away at break-neck speed but was unable to maintain the pace and ran out of gas. When, during a boisterous battle in which fortunes fluctuated, Taylor caught him with a really good punch, Lennie fell down and was too exhausted to rise.

The fight lived up to all expectations and the crowd were roaring their hearts out from the time the two young gladiators entered the ring to the final blow.

There were fantastic scenes as Taylor left the ring. His fans almost fought to get close enough to him to pat his back and it was only with great difficulty that a path was cleared through the crowd to his dressing room.

Williams was so anxious to get to grips with his rival that he danced out into the centre of the ring before the timekeeper had set the bout in motion and twice referee Harry Gibbs had to order him back to his corner to wait for the bell.

When they were gonged into action Williams waded in wildly and took Taylor out of his stride. Frank, himself a slugger fought back furiously and when the bout was only a few seconds old they were hammering away at each other.

That's how it was throughout the engagement. Their meeting had been described as the "war of the unbeatens" and that's how they treated it. The battle was fought in a white-hot atmosphere.

Williams was twice warned for borderline punches in the first round. Tough Taylor was not hurt, did not complain, and we thought that two warnings so early in a good contest was a little premature.

The Welshman did not seem to be unsettled by the voice of authority, for he plunged straight back into the battle. Taylor, who was forced to use the ring, slammed back at him and stopped him in his tracks with fierce left hooks to the head, followed swiftly by two fine right crosses that hurt Williams.

In the second round the third man warned Williams to be careful with his head, but Lennie probably did not hear him. He was so intent on bulldozing Taylor out of the fight and out of the ring if necessary.

As Lennie lunged forward, Frank whipped home a series of crisp rights to the jaw that shook Lennie. Taylor fans urged him to go in again but Williams seemed as though he was wound up clock-work style.

As Taylor`s punches put him off course, he swayed, got back on course again and was in there with two hands pumping away at Frank`s head and body.

Taylor was the more skilful of the two. Although he had to hop around, he was watching his target and placing his punches better. Frank had a feeling that Lennie might blow himself up and he was just waiting for the opportunity to present itself.

Frank had the better of the first two rounds but persistent Williams had another spurt in the third and we thought he came out on top in a non-stop punching session.

Williams scored with a good left hook to the body that bothered Taylor, but Frank stuck to his guns and he, too, was well on target with some good body blows that seemed to sap Lennie`s strength.

In the fourth round Williams slowed down. He allowed Taylor to dominate the scoring and his punches lacked fire and power. Now, we thought, Lennie had blown up. Three fierce, non-stop rounds had been his limit.

But Lennie stormed back for the fifth, which was probably his best round. The odds, which had slightly favoured Taylor at the start of the fight, had widened in the fourth. Now they shifted again, as a result of Lennie`s new lease of life. Taylor, who had earlier received a nick under the right eye, now had a cut over the eye.

It looked dangerous for Frank. Sensing the chance of an inside the distance victory, Williams threw everything he had at his man.

He caught Taylor with an assortment of lefts and right hooks and swings to the head and body and Frank was fighting desperately to keep the young Welshman at bay."

But Lennie had spent himself in that final fling. In the sixth round he was extremely tired, and Taylor knew it.

A well placed jab made the Welshman`s nose bleed and Lennie was quickly running out of breath. His mouth was open and he was becoming slower and slower.

As he stumbled from a left hook to the jaw, Taylor, urged on by his fans smashed home the perfect right cross.

Lennie went down, but with great determination he tried in vain to beat the count of Harry Gibbs. Sadly, it was not to be Lennie`s night and this was his first taste of defeat in twentynine contests, but it was vital that this bitter disappointment should be put to one side and he needed to rebound quickly.

Ron Olver writing in his weekly "Telefight News" column in Boxing News expressed his concern at the edited film of the contest shown on the BBC`s Sportsview programme. He had Lennie ahead at the end of the fifth round and felt that the film omitted much of the Welshman`s good work thereby giving the impression that Taylor was skating it, which was certainly not the case. Ron continued: "Manager Benny Jacobs too, was astounded at the misleading impression created by this film, and is not content to let the matter rest there." Benny felt that the film not only misled the public but that it was also unfair to Lennie and to any promoter who might use him in future. He stated that he would be writing to the BBC and the British Boxing Board of Control in an attempt to ensure that coverage of any contest should at least be balanced.

At the end of the night Lennie was able to leave the Royal Albert Hall virtually unmarked while Taylor was having to receive medical attention and this shows the price that the winner sometimes has to pay in a boxing ring.

There were suggestions that Lennie`s preparation had been less than ideal, and in retrospect this was a gross understatement. About a month before the contest Lennie and his wife Gloria had gone up to London for a weekend with Lennie having to present prizes at Vauxhall on the Friday evening. When he returned to the house of his wife`s aunt in Kilburn everything was locked and in darkness. It turned out that his wife, who had been expecting a baby, had suffered a miscarriage and had been rushed into hospital at Paddington. Her condition was serious but on the Saturday morning Lennie received a telegram from Benny stating that the contest with Taylor had been confirmed and that he should phone his manager immediately. He was able to return to Cardiff on the Monday and turned up at the gym in the evening weighing 10st. 4lbs. Incredibly, in a week he dropped his weight to 8st. 12 _ lbs but the worry relating to his wife's health prevented him from focussing properly on the task facing him and he returned to London the following weekend to visit his wife who was still in hospital having developed toxaemia.

In reality, this placed a sporting defeat in perspective, but ultimately it was important that Lennie should not dwell on the Taylor setback and he was back in action at Nottingham at the end of May when he beat Al Rocca once again on points over eight rounds. Rocca was the only man to have gone the distance with both the "Lion" and the "Tiger" and gave both of them a lot of trouble. The contest, promoted by Reg King at the Ice Stadium was the chief –support to the British Middleweight Championship battle between George Aldridge and Mick Leahy which saw Leahy stop the champion in the first round to take the title.

A rematch with Frankie Taylor was high on the agenda of all concerned and this was secured by promoter Harry Levene. Many fans came away from their first encounter convinced that it was the "Fight of the Year" while referee Harry Gibbs maintained it was one of the finest fights he had ever handled. As a referee I know I am expected to be able to pinpoint the winner at any moment during a contest, but Gibbs, in his autobiography "Box On" wrote: "I defy anyone to tell me who was in front after five rounds". It turned out to be a remarkable promotion with Levene securing the eagerly awaited contest between Billy Walker and Johnny Prescott, two of the country's most exciting young heavyweights. This fight was always going to be a treat for the fans with Walker's big punching and Prescott's boxing skills providing the ideal mix. As they went into the final round it seemed that Prescott might be ahead but the big-punching Walker had the final say, flooring Prescott and forcing referee Tommy Little to intervene with just 84 seconds remaining. The show also featured the training routine of World Heavyweight Champion Sonny Liston and with many fans left without tickets for the first encounter between the "Lion" and the "Tiger", Wembley was the chosen setting.

A superb picture of the weigh-in shows Lennie and Frankie together with their respective handlers and Terry Hall with his puppet, the original "Lion" made famous by television appearances, with the forbidding figure of Sonny Liston overseeing the whole affair.

Lennie was determined to approach the rematch in a cooler manner and was dictating the pattern of the contest. In Lennie's words: "I felt I had him on toast", but in the fourth round disaster struck. Lennie threw one of his fierce trademark left hooks to the body which caught Taylor at the top of the hip and Lennie felt his hand go immediately and the harsh reality dawned that the contest was over and he was left with no option but to retire at the end of the round.

Lennie was out of the ring for nine months and sought the advice of a specialist in London who suggested an operation to fuse bones in his wrist. Had he gone along with this the restricted movement would undoubtedly have meant the end of his boxing career and so Benny and Lennie learned to live with the problem by ensuring some particularly careful hand wrapping.

He returned to action in Cardiff on June 30th, 1964 when he was matched with Billy Thomas of Caerphilly for the Welsh Featherweight Title. Promoter Phil Edwards was delighted by the fact that tickets were being snapped up so quickly for this contest, which had really captured the imagination of Welsh fight fans. Billy was a great character who could have achieved a great deal, but in many ways he sacrificed much of his own career to take on the role of sparring partner to Howard Winstone and his work in this respect was greatly valued. Billy was totally overwhelmed by Lennie and was stopped in the third round with the "Lion" claiming the vacant title.

Lennie prepared for the contest sparring with gym-mates Ron Lendrum, Darkie Hughes and Geoff Rees while Billy, managed by the larger than life figure of Mac Williams sparred with Glyn Davies, Terry Gale and Howard Winstone.

The Drill Hall in Cardiff was packed to capacity when the bell rang for this contest and it was all over when the clock reached two minutes 55 seconds of round three. Lennie received a huge welcome as he entered the ring and many pundits doubted whether the courage of Billy could take him past the third round.

Once Lennie struck with his first decisive combination towards the end of the first round, his superiority was obvious and it was only a matter of time before Lennie would break down the speedy but cool-boxing Thomas. Billy boxed behind a peek-a-boo defence but was forced to the ropes by Lennie`s whirlwind attack, though for the moment, Billy was able to jab Lennie away and avoid danger.

The report in "Boxing News" continues: "Lennie had to stretch to connect and several times took combination punches to the face. Then his left caught Thomas square in the midriff, staggering him as a looping Williams right bruised his left eye. Thomas was doubled up from two more blows to the solar plexus as the bell rang.

Round two saw Lennie following up his advantages with short two-fisted attacks to the head. Billy was warned by referee Billy Jones for misusing his head in a clinch.

Thomas sank his best punches of the night, two hard rights to the Lion`s ribs. But they only served to galvanise Lennie into spectacular action.

Again, just before the bell, confident Williams was well on top and had Thomas fighting a tactical retreat from stinging head blows.

Round three again fast, hard and even, then spurred on by manager Benny Jacobs` cries of "Don`t let him out", Lennie decked Billy for a count of four with at least a dozen well-aimed finishing punches.

The 1,500 crowd and Thomas` mentor Mac Williams erupted into strong protest scenes as referee Jones wrestled Lennie away from Billy`s kneeling figure, claiming he had been hit while down in a neutral corner. Thomas struggled to offer only token resistance until the referee rescued him."

Lennie had at last claimed his first professional title, but Mac Williams, ever the protective manager, lodged an official protest with the British Boxing Board of Control against the handling by Connah`s Quay referee Billy Jones. After watching a film of the fight he claimed that his man had been hit illegally at least four times but the response of Benny Jacobs was that "Its hard to check a cluster of blows once it has been launched" and Lennie was now able to savour the fact that he was Featherweight Champion of Wales.

Lennie was in action again in September, this time in Manchester where he beat Bobby Davies on points over ten rounds but, again plagued by injury, there was to be only one contest in 1965, and this was a draw over eight rounds at Wolverhampton with Brian Cartwright who was already establishing himself as one of Britain`s leading featherweights. Benny Jacobs, knowing that Dai Corp had boxed Cartwright, asked Dai to spar with Lennie during his preparation. One of those sessions was set for 9am on a Sunday morning. Dai arrived in good time but there was no sign of Lennie. Eventually another member of the stable turned up and Dai decided to have a go at picking the lock with a nail-file rather than be standing outside. As soon as they got in they began to warm up. A few minutes later Benny arrived and with a bewildered look on his face inquired as to Lennie`s whereabouts. Dai replied that he had not seen Lennie, who had his own key to the gym. When Benny asked how they had entered Dai admitted to picking the lock. Benny, with typical humour asked why Dai was involved with boxing when a lucrative living could be made elsewhere!

 The contest with Cartwright took place on the day after Lennie`s 21st birthday and he was presented with a cake by the promoter in the company of British Lightheavyweight Champion Chic Calderwood and the American Freddie Mack whose contest topped the bill. Mack was a tough fighter and he knocked Calderwood out in the eighth round.

Several months of inactivity meant that Lennie, who had been rated number one in the featherweight rankings now slipped out of the top ten. He was determined to re-establish himself and when he was fit and ready to return to action Lennie insisted that Benny should get him a contest against the top rated fighter, who at this time just happened to be Brian Cartwright. The contest took place at Solihull on May 4th, 1966 and was staged by promoter Alex Griffiths. Lennie was in impressive form and beat Cartwright convincingly on points over eight rounds showing once more that he was a force to be reckoned with.

In September, he was in action at Carmarthen in a defence of his Welsh title against Billy Thomas and was in devastating form, this time knocking Billy out in the second round.

Frankie Taylor, who for some time had combined his fistic skills with his journalistic skills by providing a weekly column for "The People", had long been talked of as a possible challenger for Howard Winstone`s British and European titles. In fact, there were many who fancied his chances and in June 1965 he stopped the durable George Bowes of Hartlepool in six rounds in a final eliminator, but in July, Frankie faced Dominica`s Carlos Cruz and lost on points over ten rounds. Sadly, losing the contest was not the most difficult thing to accept, for an accidental clash of heads resulted in double vision. He boxed twice in 1966 but tragically had to accept that his ring career, which at one time had promised so much, was over.

This meant that the opportunity to challenge Winstone fell to Lennie. The contest was a natural for Wales and Benny Jacobs wasted no time in banging the drum on Lennie`s behalf, making no secret of the fact that he thought his man was well capable of dealing with Howard. There was a good deal of interest from London promoters but the contest was finally secured for the Afan Lido, Aberavon, by Moss Goodman of the Wyvern Sporting Club, Manchester and with Les Roberts as the matchmaker. Les, the matchmaker at the National Sporting Club, was no stranger to Wales having worked at this venue many times in the same capacity for Eddie Thomas while Benny`s legendary negotiating skills ensured that Lennie earned considerably more from the contest than did Howard, whose purse was reported to be less than £1,000.

Lennie trained extremely hard for this contest and was convinced that his power would be too much for Howard, but, as Peter Wilson wrote in the Daily Mirror: "Once more Howard Winstone proved last night that as far as Britain- and probably all Europe- is concerned, he is in a different class to all other featherweights". Interestingly, Wilson went on to express the view that: "Although Winstone won so comfortably, I would say he`s not quite the fighter he was some two years ago."

Referee Bill Williams stopped the contest with just thirty seconds remaining of the eighth round. At the time, Lennie was behind on points and seemingly unable to land the big punch that might just have turned things in his favour. True to form, Benny complained bitterly about the stoppage, especially since it was a championship contest and Lennie, too, found the decision difficult to accept claiming that he had not been on the floor, and had never been in trouble but he was the first to acknowledge Howard as a great champion.

There was talk of Lennie meeting Jimmy Anderson at the Royal Albert Hall, with the match being made at 9st 4lb, but a week before the contest Lennie was told he would have to come in at least three pounds lighter. He refused to go through with the contest and decided to retire from the sport, while Anderson was then matched with the tough Nigerian Rafiu King and was knocked out in the fifth round.

Lennie enjoyed a remarkable career and was only beaten by two men, namely Frankie Taylor and Howard Winstone. It is clear that his wife`s illness and injury contributed to his defeats against Taylor, a fighter of the highest calibre, but in Howard, he came up against a man who dominated the division for much of the sixties. Winstone was unlucky to have come up against a champion of the calibre of Vicente Saldivar while Lennie was unlucky to have come up against Howard. Ultimately, he had to be satisfied with his Welsh Title, but in any other era Lennie would almost certainly have gone on to greater things.

Lennie Williams

Featherweight
Maesteg
Born: February 2nd, 1944

1961

Jan 19	Steve Regan	Cardiff	w.rsc.1
Feb 21	Chris Dodds	Wolverhampton	w.ko.1
Mar 6	Bobby Fiddes	Maesteg	w.rsc.3
Jun 21	Gerry Jones	Cardiff	w.pts.6
Jul 11	Norman Swales	Wembley	w.rsc.1
Aug 24	Arnold Bell	Liverpool Stad.	w.rsc.3
Sep 5	Billy Williams	Wolverhampton	w.pts.6
Sep 11	Gerry Jones	Cardiff	w.ko.1
Oct 2	Alan Branquet	Maesteg	w.rsc.2
Oct 25	Tommy McMillan	Cardiff	w.rsc.1
Nov 21	John Joe Donaghy	London	w.ko.2
Nov 28	Frank Lannion	Wolverhampton	w.ko.5
Dec 4	Micky Redmond	Maesteg	w.rsc.2

1962

Jan 9	Billy Evans	Wolverhampton	w.pts.6
Jan 29	Ron Rowley	Cardiff	w.ko.3
Feb 12	Frank Lannion	Maesteg	w.rtd.5
Mar 6	Jack Dillon	Seymour Hall	w.rsc.2
Mar 20	Billy Williams	Wolverhampton	w.rtd.5
Jun 29	George O`Neill	Corwen	w.rtd.2
Jul 9	Billy Williams	Carmarthen	w.rsc.2
Aug 2	Billy Evans	Cardiff	w.rsc.3
Aug 18	George Hand	Newtown	w.rtd.4
Sep 3	Barry Ridge	Maesteg	w.rsc.4
Sep 26	Al Rocca	Solihull	w.pts.8
Dec 12	Tommy Atkins	Blackpool	w.pts.8

1963

Jan 22	Dele Majeke	Smethwick	w.ko.2
Jan 29	Jimmy Carson	Olympia	w.ko.2
Feb 27	Tommy Atkins	Blackburn	w.rsc.1
Apl 9	Frankie Taylor	Royal Albert Hall	l.ko.6
May 28	Al Rocca	Nottingham	w.pts.8
Sep 10	Frankie Taylor	Wembley	l.rtd.4

1964

Jun 30	Billy Thomas	Cardiff	w.rsc.3
	(Vacant Welsh Featherweight Title)		
Sep 10	Bobby Davies	Manchester	w.pts.10

1965

Feb 3	Brian Cartwright	Wolverhampton	d.pts.8

1966

May 4	Brian Cartwright	Solihull	w.pts.8
Sep 12	Billy Thomas	Carmarthen	w.ko.2
	(Welsh Featherweight Title)		
Dec 7	Howard Winstone	Aberavon	l.rsc.8
	(British and European Featherweight Titles)		

Lennie Williams

Lennie in the gym.
pic: Tommy Rees

Howard Winstone (left) v Lennie Williams.
pic: Courtesy of Western Mail

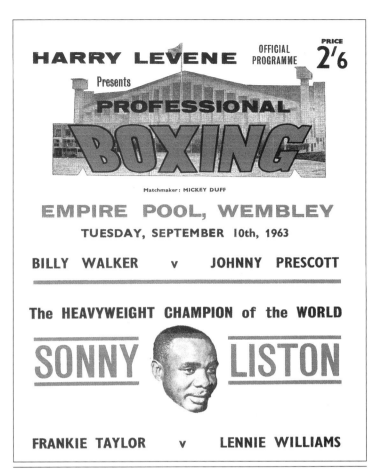

Fight Programme 1963

Frankie "Tiger" Taylor and Lennie "The Lion" Williams weigh-in.

Chapter 15

Dennis Pleace made his professional debut on April 17th, 1962 at the age of seventeen at Shoreditch Town Hall. A former Junior ABA Champion, Dennis was looked after by Benny with heavyweight brother Roger taking out a Trainer/Second licence to begin with. When he became eligible for a manager`s licence, Roger took charge but Benny took over again during the latter stages of Dennis`s career.

Sharing the stage with stablemate Johnny Furnham, who won in the sixth round when his opponent Eddie Cole was disqualified, Dennis showed a maturity beyond his years in terms of defensive technique and forced his opponent Teddy Beeston to retire in three rounds.

Between April and November he engaged in a dozen contests with just three going the distance. His punching power was such that early stoppages were secured in each of the other contests. The pace slackened in 1963 when he boxed just five times but he remained unbeaten and his confidence was sky-high as he stopped Peter Morgan in the fifth round in Cardiff on February 10th, 1964 and scoring arguably his best win to date in November when he beat Don Davies on points over six rounds.

He tasted defeat for the first time in his twentieth contest. Dennis was matched with Ricky Porter of Swindon on February 18th, 1965 at the Drill Hall in Cardiff on a bill topped by Carl Gizzi against Len "Rocky" James in an eight round heavyweight tussle which was far from a classic and ended in a points win for Gizzi.

Dennis started well enough and caught Porter with some solid, swinging blows but he was covered in blood from the first round with a bad nose-bleed. Pleace was guilty of persistent low blows which brought repeated warnings from the referee.

Porter was floored for a count of eight in the second round but Dennis was unable to finish his man off. Both men gave everything and waded into each other, but in the heat of battle, Dennis landed two low punches in the sixth round and was disqualified.

He returned to action in November in Cardiff and demolished Yvon Jarrett inside a round. He was in action at Bristol just a fortnight later and stopped Johnny Fuller in the fourth round suggesting that his career was back on track, but he registered just two wins and a draw in 1966 with losses coming against Andy Wyper, Henry Turkington and Pat Dwyer. These were opponents of genuine quality. Wyper had won the ABA Lightmiddleweight title in 1963 while

Turkington was a tough Irish fighter who mixed in the best of company. He boxed the likes of Harry Scott, Johnny Pritchett, Mark Rowe and Bunny Sterling and when I refereed him at the end of his career he was still capable of seriously testing up and coming fighters. Moments of humour in the ring are rare but I remember him complaining to me about the heat shortly before I stopped his contest against Gareth "Tashy" Jones. Pat Dwyer won the ABA Lightmiddleweight title in 1965 and he too, was a highly rated fighter, so there was no disgrace in dropping points decisions to men of this calibre.

Things looked good for Dennis in June 1967 when he beat Johnny Kramer of West Ham on points at Ninian Park on the Winstone/Saldivar undercard. Kramer held the Southern Area Middleweight title for two and a half years before losing it to future British Champion Bunny Sterling. The Cardiff man took the decision over eight rounds though he ended the fight with a nasty gash on his left cheek.

Wins followed over Len Gibbs and Tom Bell in 1968 before he faced Gibbs for the second time at the Colston Hall in Bristol in October. Brother Roger says that by this time Dennis was not the most diligent of trainers and was into the habit of taking things casually as he was earning well as a barrow-boy.

Dennis weighed in at 11st. 9.1/2lbs with Gibbs coming in at 11st. 1.1/2lbs and consequently had to pay a £25 penalty and according to "Boxing News", he "then threw away the fight which he had well in hand, by sheer recklessness," when he was disqualified in the third round.

Dennis went out for a quick win and caught Gibbs with a big right in the first round, and although the Jamaican boxed cleverly in the next round, he ran into big trouble in the third.

Gibbs went down from a combination of pushes and punches and took three short counts, but Dennis was warned by referee Harry Gibbs. When Gibbs tumbled again he appeared to have been struck on the canvas as Dennis became over-anxious. Len had no chance of beating the count but again, according to "Boxing News", "Pleace`s high spirits were dampened when the referee waved him to his corner and awarded the fight to Gibbs who was in the process of being revived as he lay full length on the floor of the ring."

On July 2nd, 1969 Dennis was matched against Carl Thomas for the Welsh Middleweight title Thomas had won against Roy John, six months earlier. The bill featured a second Welsh title fight when Glyn Davies faced Steve Curtis for the Welsh Bantamweight crown. Steve, trained by Roy Agland, created a huge impression by taking the title on points in what was only his fifth professional contest. Both these contests saw Benny Jacobs pitted against Mac Williams and in truth it was a terrific bill with heavyweight Dennis Avoth producing a barnstorming finish to earn a draw against Del Phillips. Indeed, the disqualification of Dennis Pleace brought the only sour note to the whole evening.

Potentially, the match between Pleace and Thomas was a cracker, but just as the action was warming up, the end came abruptly in the third round with Pleace being disqualified.

Thomas was caught by a fierce right and went down in Pleace`s corner. Dennis was unable to contain himself and rushed in, landing another right into

Thomas`s side as he was on the canvas. Carl did not get up and referee Adrian Morgan indicated that the fight was over, with Thomas still holding the title.

Roger Pleace described it as a disgusting decision and felt that Thomas had stayed down deliberately, but Mac Williams, Carl`s manager, insisted that his man was hurt by a blow to the kidney area when Thomas was down and felt that the referee had no alternative but to disqualify Pleace.

On January 19th, 1970 Dennis was matched with Bunny Sterling at the Anglo American Sporting Club in an eliminator for the British Middleweight title but the Cardiff man paid the penalty for inactivity as he ran out of steam in what was only his second contest in fourteen months.

Referee Harry Gibbs intervened half way through the ninth round and there were derisory cheers when it was announced that "the referee stops the contest to save Pleace from further punishment".

Pleace had dished out his fair share of punishment earlier in the contest and was close to a stoppage win in the fourth round with his ruthless body punching. A huge body shot dumped Sterling on the lower rope, but when he tried to follow up with a similar delivery he was warned for a low blow.

Significantly, it was only during the second half of the contest that Sterling was able to dominate and the accuracy of his left jab drew blood from the nose of Pleace.

There was excitement in the Welsh corner when Dennis floored Sterling with a superb short right for a count of four but from then on he was never in any real danger.

After the fight Dennis admitted that even though he may have looked fit he needed to fight more often while Benny and cornerman Phil Edwards expressed the hope that Dennis would be boxing again in about five weeks.

Unfortunately the next contest did not materialise and Dennis Pleace retired without perhaps realising his potential. He was undoubtedly a devastating puncher and lost some of his contests through indiscipline when he was within a whisker of stunning victory. Flame coloured hair and a fiery temperament are often said to go together, but with a more measured approach Dennis could well have become a champion.

Dennis Pleace

Lightmiddle/Middleweight
Cardiff
Born: March 14, 1945

1962

Apr 17	Teddy Beeston	London	w.rtd.3
May 1	Fitzroy Lindo	London	w.rsc.2
May 15	Jim Smith	Maesteg	w.ko.1
May 30	Teddy Gardner	Cardiff	w.rsc.2
Jun 19	Eddie Obermuller	Bristol	w.rsc.3
Jun 29	Jimmy Mitchell	Corwen	w.rtd.2
Jul 9	Obie Hayward	Carmarthen	w.ko.3
Aug 2	Terry Phillips	Cardiff	w.dis.5
Aug 18	Johnny Dolphin	Newtown	w.pts.6
Sep 26	Ray Raheem	Solihull	w.pts.6
Oct 1	Terry Phillips	Cardiff	w.pts.6
Nov 20	Billy Allport	Leicester	w.rsc.2

1963

Jan 16	Ray Raheem	Leicester	w.rsc.2
May 8	Wally Williams	Blackpool	w.pts.6
Aug 10	Steve Ako	Newtown	w.rsc.4
Sep 10	Harry Wheeler	Wembley	w.ko.2
Oct 7	Steve Ako	Maesteg	w.pts.8

1964

Feb 10	Peter Morgan	Cardiff	w.rsc.5
Nov 25	Don Davis	London	w.pts.6

1965

Feb 18	Ricky Porter	Cardiff	l.dis.6
Nov 25	Yvon Jarrett	Cardiff	w.rsc.1
Dec 6	Johnny Fuller	Bristol	w.rsc.4

1966

Mar 21	Tom Bell	London	d.8
Apr 18	Andy Wyper	London	l.pts.8
May 15	Young Cassius	London	w.pts.8
Jun 14	Henry Turkington	Wembley	l.rsc.5
Aug 6	Pat Dwyer	London	l.pts.8
Sep 26	Brian Gale	Bristol	w.rsc.3

1967

Apr 26	Bob Cofie	Porthcawl	l.pts.8
Jun 15	Johnny Kramer	Cardiff	w.pts.8

1968

Jan 22	Len Gibbs	London	w.rsc.6
Feb 12	Tom Bell	London	w.pts.8
Oct 21	Len Gibbs	Bristol	l.dis.3
Oct 28	Sugar Bill Robinson	London	w.rsc.2

1969

Jul 2	Carl Thomas	Cardiff	l.dis.3
	(Welsh Middleweight Title)		

1970

Jan 19	Bunny Sterling	AASC, London	l.rsc.9
	(Elim. British Middleweight Title)		

DENNIS PLEACE
CARDIFF
Manager: BENNY JACOBS   Photo: TOMMY REES
COPYRIGHT

Dennis Pleace

Selected Records

Eddie Bee
Steve Curtis
Peter Delbridge
Johnny Furnham
Len Harvey
Roland Hicks
Gene Innocent
Len "Rocky" James
Gerald Kitchen
Ron Lendrum
Ebe Mensah
Geoff Rees
Brian Renney
Johnny Thomas

Eddie Bee

Welterweight
Cardiff
Born: Trinidad, April 8th, 1934

1956

Jun 18	Tommy Enifer	Birmingham	w.ko.2
Jul 7	Beau Griffiths	Aberystwyth	w.ko.4
Jul 26	Gerry Bedford	Liverpool Stad.	w.pts.4
Aug 23	Tommy Barnabas	Liverpool Stad	w.pts.4
Oct 1	Tommy Barnabas	Walsall	w.ko.3
Oct 11	Tex Woodward	Birmingham	l.pts.6
Oct 23	Johnny Griffin	Willenhall	w.pts.6
Nov 12	Eddie Williams	Cardiff	w.pts.6

1957

May 17	Tex Woodward	Belle Vue, Man.	l.pts.6
May 28	Derek Liversidge	Doncaster	l.rtd.6
Jun 21	Don Martin	Manchester	w.rsc.5
Jul 25	Tommy Keeley	Liverpool Stad.	l.pts.6
Aug 21	Teddy Barrow	Cross Keys	w.ko.4
Sep 9	Teddy Barker	Maindy Stadium	w.ko.1
Sep 18	Leo Molloy	Pontypridd	l.pts.8
Oct 28	Boswell St. Louis	Birmingham	l.rtd.5

1958

Mar 2	Johnny Plenty	Haverfordwest	w.rsc.2
Apr 3	Tommy Tagoe	Birmingham	l.rsc.4
Jul 22	Johnny Plenty	Oswestry	w.ko.2
Sep 3	Teddy Barrow	Coney Beach	w.rsc.2
Dec 6	Paddy McAuley	Belfast	w.rsc.4

1959

Feb 2	Mick Leahy	Coventry	l.pts.8
May 4	Tony Smith	Belle Vue, Man.	l.rsc.8
Aug 8	Terry Burnett	Ebbw Vale	l.pts.8
Sep 14	Sandy Manuel	Ebbw Vale	l.pts.8

Steve Curtis

Bantamweight
Cardiff
Born: December 26th, 1948
Died: October 28th, 1994
Welsh ABA Flyweight Champion, 1967, 1968

1968

Nov 11	John Kellie	NSC	d.pts.6
Nov 26	Jim Henry	Belfast	l.rsc.8

1969

Feb 4	Johnny Fitzgerald	Bristol	w.pts.6
Mar 17	Sammy Vernon	NSC	w.pts.6
Jul 2	Glyn Davies	Cardiff	w.pts.10
	(Vacant Welsh Bantamweight Title)		
Sep 29	Glyn Davies	NSC	w.pts.10
Dec 1	Orizu Obilaso	Derby	l.ko.2

Steve Curtis

Peter Delbridge

Featherweight
Cardiff
Born: July 12th, 1934

1959

Nov 23	Chris Elliott	Banbury	l.pts.6

1960

Mar 14	Mickey Redmond	Leyton Baths	w.pts.6
Mar 31	Trevor Jenkins	Cardiff	w.rsc.5
Apr 6	Aubrey Day	Wolverhampton	l.pts.6
Jul 13	Kenny Field	Shoreditch	l.pts.6
Jul 27	Mickey Redmond	Coney Beach	w.pts.6
Aug 19	Mickey Redmond	Banbury	l.pts.6
Aug 29	Brian Smith	Coney Beach	l.pts.6
Sep 12	Billy Secular	NSC	l.pts.6
Oct 25	Al McCarthy	Wembley	l.rsc.3
Nov 25	Mickey Redmond	Cheltenham	l.pts.6

1961

Mar 14	Billy Davis	Shoreditch	l.rtd.2
Oct 2	Ron Rowley	Maesteg	w.pts.6
Oct 10	Bobby Davies	Finsbury Park	l.ko.2
Oct 25	Ron Rowley	Cardiff	w.pts.6
Dec 4	Peter Richards	Maesteg	w.pts.6

1962

Jan 29	Dai Harris	Cardiff	l.rsc.5

Peter Delbridge

Johnny Furnham

Middleweight
Cardiff
Born: January 25th, 1939

1961

Feb 21	Roland Mitchell	Wolverhampton	w.rtd.2
Mar 6	Herbie Williams	Maesteg	w.ko.3
Mar 27	Roland Mitchell	NSC	w.rsc.3
Apr 4	Simon Emu	Wolverhampton	w.pts.6
May 2	Jimmy Assani	Wembley	l.pts.6
May 12	Roy McArthur	Manchester	w.rsc.4
Jun 21	Johnny Gribble	Cardiff	w.rsc.4
Sep 11	Ivor Delima	Cardiff	w.rsc.2
Oct 2	Johnny Plenty	Maesteg	w.pts.6
Nov 20	Eddie Phillips	Nottingham	w.pts.6
Nov 28	Sid Brown	Wolverhampton	w.rtd.4
Dec 4	Tony French	Maesteg	l.pts.8
Dec 19	Lloyd Lewis	Merthyr	w.ko.3

1962

Jan 9	Teddy Gardner	Wolverhampton	w.ko.4
Feb 26	Gordon White	Merthyr	l.rsc.2
Mar 20	Dave Wakefield	Wolverhampton	w.pts.4
Apr 17	Eddie Cole	Shoreditch	w.dis.6
May 8	Tommy Hayes	Treorchy	w.pts.8

Johnny Furnham representing Wales in an Amateur International.

Len Harvey

Featherweight
Cardiff
Born: December 16th, 1933

1957

Mar 4	John O`Brien	Newcastle	l.pts.6
Mar 11	Billy Adams	Walsall	l.pts.6
May 16	George Carroll	Liverpool Stad.	l.pts.6
May 30	Peter Reed	Norwich	d.pts.6
Jun 15	Gil Neill	Belfast	l.pts.8
Aug 15	Owen Reilly	Kelvin Hall, Glasgow	l.pts.8
Aug 24	Billy Anderson	Corwen	d.pts.4
Sep 2	Terry Sherran	Maesteg	w.pts.4
Oct 1	Terry Brown	Shoreditch	w.rsc.5
Oct 21	Ivan McCready	Maindy Stadium	l.pts.8
Oct 28	Johnny Kidd	Leyton Baths	l.pts.6

1958

Jan 27	Johnny Fitzpatrick	Banbury	w.ko.1
Feb 17	Aubrey Day	Kettering	l.pts.8
Mar 21	Tommy Williams	Haverfordwest	l.pts.8
Mar 31	Paddy Kelly	Londonderry	w.ko.4
Apr 12	George O`Neill	Belfast	l.pts.8
May 23	Paddy Kelly	Ballymena	l.pts.8
Jun 28	Floyd Robertson	Belfast	l.pts.8
Oct 6	Fred Bancroft	Maesteg	w.pts.8
Nov 12	Tommy Williams	Cardiff	l.pts.6
Nov 18	Dave Stone	Shoreditch	l.rsc.6
Dec 6	Jim Jordan	Belfast	l.pts.8

1959

Apr 3	Colin Salcombe	Banbury	l.pts.8
Jun 24	Terry Rees	Coney Beach	l.pts.8
Sep 22	Johnny Butch Davis	Shoreditch	l.pts.6
Nov 10	Tommy Tiger	Bristol	l.pts.6

1960

Feb 2	Tony Icke	Walsall	l.pts.6
Mar 22	Alan Howard	West Ham Baths	d.pts.6
Apr 6	Terry Edwards	Wolverhampton	l.pts.6
Jul 16	Terry McManus	Cork, Ireland	l.pts.6

Len Harvey

Roland Hicks

Middleweight
Cardiff

1957

Oct 28	Mickey Davis	Wembley Town Hall	l.rsc.3

1958

Mar 21	Tommy Masebo	Haverfordwest	l.pts.6
Oct 6	Norman Jenkins	Maesteg	l.pts.6
Nov 12	Tommy Masebo	Cardiff	w.pts.6

1959

Mar 9	Ray Ward	Halifax	w.ko.4
Aug 22	Terry Lake	Colwyn Bay	w.pts.6

Roland Hicks

Gene Innocent

Heavyweight
Cardiff
Born: January 4th, 1945

1967

May 10	Mick Carter	Solihull	w.rsc.1
Jun 13	Jimmy McIlvane	Wolverhampton	w.pts.6
Sep 27	Barry Rodney	Solihull	w.pts.6
Oct 19	Jimmy McIlvaney	Bristol	w.rsc.2
Nov 28	Peter Thomas	Bristol	w.rsc.3
Dec 20	Jimmy McIlvaney	London	w.rsc.4

1968

Feb 20	Paul Brown	Wolverhampton	w.rsc.3
Mar 26	Len Rocky James	Birmingham	w.co.3
May 13	Ernie Field	Manchester	w.rtd.2
Nov 12	Joe Bugner	Wembley	l.rsc.3

1969

Jan 15	Guinea Roger	Solihull	l.rsc.4
Apr 1	Frank Poleon	AASC	l.rsc.2

1972

Oct 4	Roger Barlow	Caerphilly	d.pts.6

1973

Feb 5	Mal Isaacs	Swansea	w.co.1
Jun 27	Dennis Avoth	Swansea	l.pts.10
	(Vacant Welsh Heavyweight Title)		
Aug 1	Mal Isaacs	Cardiff	w.rsc.3
Nov 27	Peter Freeman	Blackpool	l.pts.10

Gene Innocent
pic: the collection of David Furnish

Len "Rocky" James

Heavyweight
Bristol
Born: February 7th, 1933
Welsh ABA Heavyweight Champion, 1962

1963

May 8	Charlie White	Blackpool	w.dis.3
Aug 10	Mick Basten	Newtown	l.pts.6
Dec 2	Len Hobbs	Manor Place Baths	l.pts.6

1964

Feb 10	Len Hobbs	Cardiff	l.pts.6
Oct 27	Billy Wynter	Wembley	w.pts.6
Dec 1	Jim Monaghan	Belfast	w.dis.5
Dec 15	Ron Gray	Wolverhampton	l.rsc.5

1965

Feb 18	Carl Gizzi	Cardiff	l.pts.8
Mar 30	Billy Wynter	Wembley	l.pts.6
Jun 28	Carl Gizzi	NSC	l.rsc.5
	(Welsh Heavyweight Title)		
Oct 4	Derek Groombridge	Bristol	w.pts.6
Nov 1	Dane Duric	Bristol	w.rsc.3
Dec 6	Jim Monaghan	Bristol	l.pts.8

1966

Feb 1	Mick Cowan	Blackpool	w.rsc.2
Mar 28	Ermanno Festorazzi	WSC	l.rsc.2
Sep 26	Derek Groombridge	Bristol	l.pts.6
Nov 10	Rocky Campbell	Bristol	l.ko.2

1967

Jan 17	Terry Daly	Royal Albert Hall	w.ko.3
Jan 24	Jim McIlvaney	Wolverhampton	w.pts.6
Feb 16	Doyle Brown	AASC	l.pts.6
Mar 20	Charlie Wilson	London	d.pts.8
Jun 5	Doyle Brown	London	w.ko.2
Jun 15	Roger Tighe	Ninian Park	l.pts.8
Nov 7	Billy Wynter	Wembley	l.pts.6

1968

Feb 20	Terry Daly	Royal Albert Hall	w.rsc.1
Mar 26	Gene Innocent	Birmingham	l.ko.3

Len 'Rocky' James (left) with Malcolm Collins.
pic: Courtesy of Western Mail

Gerald Kitchen

Welterweight
Cardiff
Born: June 2nd, 1940

1958

| Oct 23 | Tony Smith | Liverpool Stad. | l.rsc.6 |
| Dec 8 | Billy Keirnan | Cheltenham | w.rsc.1 |

1959

Mar 14	Norman Jenkins	Newport	l.pts.6
Apr 15	Roland Hicks	Cardiff	l.pts.6
Jun 8	Peter Anderson	London	l.pts.6
Nov 19	Mike Robbins	Cheltenham	w.pts.6

1960

| Jan 11 | Neville Axford | Cheltenham | l.pts.6 |

1961

| Nov 14 | Gus Harry | Shoreditch | w.ko.1 |
| Nov 28 | Billy Allport | Wolverhampton | d.pts.6 |

1962

| Jan 29 | Terry Phillips | Cardiff | w.pts.6 |

1964

Jun 14	John Charles	Brighton	w.pts.6
Jul 20	Wally Williams	Bristol	w.pts.6
Sep 10	Billy Bowman	Manchester	l.pts.6

Gerald Kitchen

Ron Lendrum

Bantamweight
Pontypridd
Born: July 2nd, 1938
Welsh ABA Bantamweight Champion, 1961
Welsh ABA Featherweight Champion, 1960, 1962

1963

Jul 29	Candido Sawyer	Cardiff	w.pts.6
Aug 10	Dave Johnson	Newtown	w.ko.4
Oct 7	Candido Sawyer	Maesteg	w.ko.3
Dec 2	Mick Taheny	Manor Place Baths	w.rsc.6

1964

Feb 10	Brady Barlow	Cardiff	w.pts.6
Mar 23	Brady Barlow	Brighton	w.pts.6
May 4	Johnny Coats	Cardiff	w.rsc.3
Jun 14	Carl Taylor	Brighton	l.pts.8
Dec 15	Kid Hassan	Cardiff	w.rsc.8

1962

Feb 18	Keith Tate	Cardiff	l.pts.8
Apr 27	Colin Lake	Brighton	l.pts.8

Ron Lendrum
pic: Courtesy of Ron Lendrum, Personal Collection

Ebe Mensah

Lightweight
Born: Ghana, December 28th, 1934

1956

Jan 30	Darkie Hughes	Carmarthen	l.pts.8
Mar 28	Pat McCoy	Hereford	w.pts.8
Jun 14	Ian Fraser	Wembley	w.rsc.2
Sep 24	Dennis Hinson	Oxford	w.pts.8
Oct 11	Darkie Hughes	Liverpool	w.pts.8
Nov 12	Teddy Best	Cardiff	w.pts.8

1957

Oct 14	John McNally	Newcastle	w.rsc.7
Oct 28	Andy Baird	Birmingham	d.pts.8

1958

Feb 17	Andy Baird	Cheltenham	w.rsc.3
Mar 3	Ronnie Rush	Walsall	w.rsc.5
Mar 8	Al Sharpe	Belfast	w.pts.8
Apr 2	Mario Vecchiatto	Milan	l.pts.10
May 12	Jim Spike McCormack	Great Yarmouth	w.pts.8
Sep 9	Ronnie Rush	Birmingham	d.pts.8

1959

Sep 29	Ola Michael	Leicester	w.pts.8

1960

Jul 2	Aissa Hashas	Algiers	l.ko.4
Nov 11	Jacques Chauveau	Bruay, France	w.pts.10
Nov 28	Johnny Nolan	Carmarthen	w.rsc.4
Dec 6	Maurice Cullen	Wembley	d.pts.8

1961

Jan 24	Brian Jones	Leicester	w.rtd.7
Feb 21	Maurice Cullen	Wolverhampton	l.pts.8
Jul 6	Johnny Cooke	Liverpool	l.pts.8
Oct 6	Tivador Balogh	Gothenburg	w.pts.8

1962 *Inactive*

1963

Jan 22	Dave Coventry	Finsbury Park	w.dis.2
Mar 1	Michele Gullotti	Milan	d.pts.10
Apr 23	Brian Jones	Finsbury Park	w.pts.8
Jul 30	John White	Blackpool	l.pts.8

1964

Feb 5	Fred Galiana	Barcelona	l.pts.10
Mar 5	Jim Spike McCormack	Belfast	l.pts.10
Mar 25	Nat Jacobs	Solihull	w.pts.8
Apr 3	Fred Galiana	Barcelona	l.pts.10
May 11	Fortunato Manca	Naples	l.pts.8
Sep 30	Joe Falcon	Solihull	w.pts.8
Oct 17	Willy Quatuor	Berlin	l.rsc.6

1965

Nov 1	Brian McCaffrey	Mayfair	l.rsc.6

1966

Apr 28	Brian Maunsell	Canterbury, NZ	l.rsc.10
May 19	Steve Wheeler	Canterbury, NZ	w.pts.10
Jun 11	Dennis Hagen	Invercargill, NZ	w.pts.10
Jun 23	Norm "Kid" Langford	Canterbury, NZ	w.pts.10
Jul 14	Gary Ford	Canterbury, NZ	w.pts.10

Geoff Rees

Welterweight
Cardiff
Born: January 1st, 1942
Welsh ABA Lightwelterweight Champion, 1961, 1962

1963

Feb 27	Patrick Onwuna	Blackburn	w.pts.6
Apr 9	Patrick Onwuna	Royal Albert Hall	w.rsc.1
Jun 10	Joey Burns	NSC	w.pts.6
Jun 24	Joey Burns	Carmarthen	w.rsc.1
Jul 29	Stan Bishop	Cardiff	w.pts.6
Aug 10	Tommy Tiger	Newtown	w.rsc.5
Nov 25	Gordon McAteer	Manchester	l.rsc.4

1964

Mar 3	Sugar Ray Johnson	Leicester	w.pts.6
Apr 21	John Smith	Birmingham	d.pts.6
May 4	Stan Bishop	Cardiff	w.rsc.7
Jun 30	Ricky Porter	Cardiff	w.pts.8
Oct 27	Al Downes	Wembley	d.pts.6
Nov 25	Dave Astley	Solihull	w.pts.6
Dec 15	Ricky Porter	Cardiff	l.rsc.7

1965

Jun 29	Terry Phillips	NSC	l.rsc.4
	(Vacant Welsh Welterweight Title)		

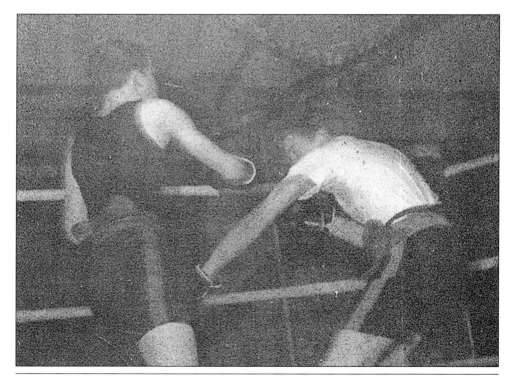

Geoff Rees (right) in action against Don James in an amateur contest.

Brian Renney

Lightweight
Cardiff
Born: January 4th, 1941
Welsh ABA Lightweight Champion, 1961, 1963

1963

May 20	Alf Leroy	London	w.rsc.3
Jul 29	Patrick Onwuma	Cardiff	w.pts.6
Aug 6	Ron Rowley	Llanelli	w.pts.6
Sep 20	Joey Burns	Corwen	w.rsc.5
Oct 7	Patrick Onwuma	Maesteg	w.pts.6
Dec 3	Eric Cartmel	London	l.ko.1

1964

Feb 10	Hugh Burke	Cardiff	w.rsc.3
May 4	Junior Lindo	Cardiff	w.ko.1
Jun 9	Don Gibson	Morecambe	w.pts.6
Jun 30	Dele Majeke	Cardiff	w.rsc.3
Sep 10	Ken Thompson	Manchester	w.dis.4
Dec 15	Billy Secular	Cardiff	w.rsc.7

1965

Jan 20	Tommy Atkins	Cardiff	w.pts.8
Mar 29	Gordon Davies	Carmarthen	l.rsc.4

Brian Renney
pic: Kindly loaned from Brian's own collection

Johnny Thomas

Bantamweight
Cardiff
Born: January 12th, 1938
Welsh ABA Bantamweight Champion,1956

1959

Jan 17	Billy Allport	Birmingham	w.pts.6
Feb 4	Dennis Everett	Cardiff	w.ko.1
Apr 3	Harry Salcombe	Banbury	w.ko.2
Apr 15	Derek Jack	Cardiff	w.ko.1
May 27	Ron Harris	Cardiff	w.ko.3
Jul 14	Ron Harris	Aberdare	w.rsc.1
Aug 22	Don Lewis	Colwyn Bay	w.rsc.3
Sep 14	Johnny Barlow	Ebbw Vale	w.pts.6
Oct 28	Peter Hibbert	Cardiff	w.rtd.2

1960

Feb 2	Frank Lannion	Walsall	w.rsc.6
May 10	Dave Caulfield	Shoreditch	w.ko.1
Jun 14	Johnny Boston	Merthyr	w.rsc.2
Jun 28	Dennis East	London	w.pts.8
Aug 15	Danny McNamee	Aberdare	w.rsc.4
Oct 11	Roy Beaman	Wembley	l.rsc.4

Johnny Thomas

Epilogue

Looking back over Benny's time in boxing his achievements were quite remarkable. Every manager dreams of managing a heavyweight champion and Joe Erskine was clearly the jewel in Benny's crown, but having said that, Phil Edwards, David "Darkie" Hughes, Harry Carroll and Lennie Williams were only defeated by the very best and showed that they belonged in championship class.

Many of Benny's boxers distinguished themselves in the amateur code, representing Wales, winning Welsh and even full ABA titles and several won Welsh titles in the professional ranks. To a man, they had all learned their trade and were capable of giving a good account of themselves. Several of them went on to train future generations of boxers while others put a great deal back into the sport by serving on the Welsh Area Council of the British Boxing Board of Control. As with Harry Carroll and David "Darkie" Hughes, Brian Renney also served on the area council and was a BBB of C Representative Steward for many years while also becoming a highly successful businessman and another who enjoyed great success in the business world was Ron Lendrum.

In the course of this book I have tried to pinpoint many of Benny's qualities including his humour, generosity and his care and affection for his fighters. What is also apparent is that all his fighters had a special affection for him in return. They all appreciated the fact that he would not take payment from them until they were all on their way in the professional ring and he was always the first to deal with medical bills. Even though he was a big gambling man he tried to discourage his fighters from becoming involved, but sadly, not always with success.

Another element which shines through is the great bond which existed between gym members and remains to this day. I was aware of this with the members of the Eddie Thomas gym and I see it now with Enzo Calzaghe's fighters. It is something which is almost unique to boxing.

Over the years, Benny emerged as a great character and enriched the sporting scene in Wales by his very understanding of the way in which the media operates. There was always a story to tell or a match to be made and he ensured that his fighters were always very much in the public eye.

During my research for this book I was struck by the almost daily coverage of boxing in the Western Mail and the South Wales Echo, a situation far-removed from present day reporting. Ironically, Welsh boxers are currently enjoying what is arguably their most successful period ever at British and world level though without the degree of coverage they perhaps deserve, but in terms of colour and personality, Benny's Boys would have held their own in any era.